THE
PURPOSE-LIVING
LEADER

God
Bless!

Paul
Bryan

THE
PURPOSE-LIVING
LEADER

A Legacy of Leadership

PAUL E. BRYANT

Wasteland Press
Shelbyville, KY USA
www.wastelandpress.net

The Purpose-Living Leader:
A Legacy of Leadership
by Paul E. Bryant

First Printing—November 2009
ISBN: 978-1-60047-377-7

Printed in the U.S.A.

I would like to thank the following people for their input, support and encouragement on this project. Each of them have given me wise counsel and support.

Robin Bryant
Brazier Bryant
Madison Bryant
Paul Bryant II
Evelyn Bryant Jones
Barry Carlson
Jim Clifton
George Fraser
Bob Gjhere
Stedman Graham
Mel Gravely
Wes Hall
Dennis Kimbro
John Kotouc
Jocelyn Perkins
Larry Robinson
Felicia Rogers
Bryan Surratt
Karen Waggoneer
Tricia Warren
Wally Weitz
Geralyn Bryant

Thank you and may God bless each and everyone of you! I appreciate your support.

A very special thanks to Steve Gordan Jr. of RDQLUS Creative for the cover design. He offers the epitome of graphic design. Thank you for your support Steve, stay creative and don't ever change!

Table of Contents

Introduction

Anyone blessed to have acquired any measure of wisdom, has certainly asked one of these questions; "What is my purpose? Why am I here and what is the meaning of life?" I've asked those questions many times, and found my answers varied according to my age and maturity. One constant, however, was my appreciation for the people in my circle. Every time I attend the funeral of someone I love I am reminded how precious and short life can be.

I've reached a reflective stage and have come to grips with my mortality. Some may say I'm going through a mid-life crisis. I choose to think of it as a normal step in the mental evolution of man. I'm transitioning into the philosophical phase...

After achieving the goals I have set for myself as a young man, I now face a crossroads. My life's ambition once followed the fast lane of money, success and prestige. I now realize all paths lead to the same destination. The next decision isn't that complicated; it boils down to what scenery I choose to view for the rest of my journey and how I will live my dash.

The summations of my feelings are in the following poem.

The Dash

I read of a man who stood to speak,
At the funeral of a friend.
He referred to the dates, on her tombstone,
From the beginning to the end.

He noted that first, came the date of her birth,
And spoke the following date with tears.

But he said what mattered most of all,
Was the dash, between those years.

For that dash represents all the time
she spent, alive upon this earth.
And now, only those who loved her,
Know what that little line is worth.

For it matters not how much we own;
The cars, the house, the cash.
What matters is how we live and love
And how we spend our dash.

So think about this long and hard.
Are there things you'd like to change?
For you never know how much time is left,
That can still be rearranged.

If we could just slow down enough,
To consider what's true and real.
And always try to understand
The way other people feel.

And be less quick to anger,
And show appreciation more
And love the people in our lives,
Like we've never loved before.

If we treat each other with respect,
And more often wear a smile.
Remembering that this special dash,
Might only last a little while.

So, when your eulogy is being read,
With your life's actions to rehash.
Would you, be proud of the things they say,
About how you spent your dash?

by Linda Ellis

There is a simple truth in this poem. The
foundation of your legacy will be established by
those you influence. The only things that really
matter are the things you do for others. Every
experience we encounter brings us closer to
discovering God's expectation for our lives. We
only need to open our eyes and ears to see and hear

the lessons of life that will chart our destiny and create our legacy.

Within this book I share events and experiences from my journey from success to significance. Like an urban Huckleberry Finn I navigated through the streets of the ghetto to become a corporate executive only to find the pot of gold at the end of the rainbow wasn't enough. I encourage you to continue reading and share a laugh or a tear at my expense. My ultimate prayer is that somewhere along the way, YOUR purpose becomes crystal clear.

Chapter One

Roots

How deep are they?

As far back as I can remember unusual events have happened to me. I can't explain it, nor predict it; things start happening and the next thing I know I'm standing in the eye of a tornado. From the backstreets to the boardrooms; from the streets to the suites, I've been there. My life is a continuous adventure crossing paths with people high in society and those least in notoriety. For years I've held on to the thought that God was leading me through these experiences for a reason.

I am extremely excited about the release of this book. I've often toyed with the prospect of writing, but my ideas never seemed to make the transformation from thoughts to words. Where I come from, drafting one's memoirs was not a common thing to do. Even though my life has been everything but ordinary, one question continually discouraged me, *"What makes you think your life is so interesting that people will want to read about it?"*

I searched to find the source of my uncertainty. Why did I doubt my experiences would interest anyone? After honest soul searching, I narrowed it down to the lack of confidence and insecurity. As much as I hate to admit it, internally I thought, *"I'm just a guy from Omaha, Nebraska; no one will care about what I have to say."*

Coming from Omaha I've grown accustomed to being taken lightly. Whenever I'm in a larger metropolitan area and I tell someone I'm from Omaha, their facial expression changes. The first response from my African American brothers and sisters is usually, *"I didn't know black people lived in Nebraska,"* and the second is usually some condescending remark.

Roots

I respond to these people in one of three ways. Sometimes I enlighten them about several of the famous people to come from Omaha. People like, Civil Rights Activist Malcolm X, NFL Hall of Fame running back Gale Sayers, Baseball Hall of Fame pitcher Bob Gibson, Olympic Gold medalist and NBA champion Bob Boozer, NBA record holder Ron Boone and Heisman Trophy winner Johnny Rodgers, Media mogul Cathy Hughes, Businessman Nathaniel Goldston, Investor Warren Buffett, President Gerald Ford, Actor John Beasley or my beautiful cousin, Actress Gabriel Union, all are from Omaha.

Other times I say nothing and just listen as they talk with pride about their city. They boast about their environment because of the sizzle of the moment. Often job relocation is the only reason they live in those cities.

Then there are times when I feel like educating. I say with pride, I'm the fifth generation of my family to live in Omaha. I explain that during the early

Roots

1900s Omaha was the national hub of the railroad and meatpacking industries. I explain how my ancestors were pioneers who moved to Omaha to seek work to provide better lives for their families.

Then I go deep on them. What they don't know is that I am a link in a very long chain, standing on broad shoulders like those of my paternal grandmother, Mildred Penny.

Grandma Mildred was a thick, brown-skinned woman with a strong personality. She stood about 5'10" and weighed around 180 pounds. Grandma was as tough as any man. She had a husky voice, a quick temper and didn't seem to care much for frilly, feminine, fashion-related things. She was not the stereotypical soft, nurturing grandmother. Grandma Mildred was impressed with hard work and accomplishment. She had disdain for lazy and weak people. If you couldn't pull your weight, your value was diminished in her eyes.

Roots

My Grandma was a smart, forceful woman who possessed a considerable amount of drive. She constantly talked about the many ways to succeed and how a strong black man would not let anything stop him from achieving.

In my earliest memories, I remember her telling me about her father. Grandma was extremely proud of her father. He was an educated black man who owned property. She constantly talked about the land he owned in Kansas. At the time, I was too young to understand the importance of that land or the significance of my grandmother's roots. My grandmother was from a city named Nicodemus, Kansas.

Nicodemus has a rich history dating to the period of "Exodus" for blacks from the Deep South. Between 1870 and 1880, former slaves fleeing racial discrimination and poverty in the South trekked north across the prairie of Kansas in search of the "Promised Land." Nicodemus, established in 1877, was the first black rural settlement in Kansas.

Roots

Today, the town of Nicodemus is the last remaining survivor of a dozen all-black Kansas settlements. It is the only remaining Western town established by African Americans during the Reconstruction Period following the Civil War. It is symbolic of the pioneer spirit of African Americans who dared to leave the South to seek personal freedom and opportunity.

Nicodemus was declared a National Historic Landmark in 1974 and on November 12, 1996, President Bill Clinton signed the historical designation into law.

The name, Nicodemus, was not derived from the Biblical Nicodemus. It was a tribute to a legendary slave and prophet who reportedly arrived on the second slave ship to reach America and was the first slave in this country to purchase his freedom.

Growing up in an all-black town in the early 1900s had to be extremely difficult. Only the bravest and most determined ex-slaves were the ones who took

6

Roots

the risk to come north. Those pioneers may have found freedom, but life had to be tough.

It was the type of environment where only the strong survived. This independent, self-sufficient backdrop developed within my Grandma Mildred a penchant for hard work and the desire for prosperity. The mind-set of those early pioneers was to work hard and earn their way to the top.

Growing up in Nicodemus instilled in her a spirit that said you can accomplish anything and you can overcome all odds and you must never, ever, give up. That is the spirit she passed on to me; I can hear Grandma Mildred now, she would say, *"Boy, you wrote the book, put it out there and let God use it!"*

On my grandfather's side of the family, the tree is old with very deep roots. The Bryant-Fisher Family Reunion has been held in Omaha on the second Sunday in August for over 90 years. It's an annual tradition rain or shine with well over 1,000 attendees returning to Omaha from all corners of the

7

country and over seas. I am proud to say our family reunion is recognized in the Guinness Book of World Records.

From the time I was a toddler, I can remember listening to aunts and uncles tell stories about "the old-timers" and relatives who overcame obstacles to become successful. The latest buzz is the film success of Gabrielle Union, who comes back to celebrate with us every year. This sense of history always has been a source of pride and self-respect. Bryant-Fisher's know where we come from and we know our ancestors.

My great-great-great-great-grandfather was a well-to-do white Missouri plantation owner. His favorite son, Wesley (my great-great-great-grandfather) received better treatment than many Negro slaves of that era because he looked like his father. Wesley was never treated like a slave. It wasn't uncommon during that time for a slave owner to father numerous children with his slaves.

Roots

When the Civil War erupted, Wesley (with the help of his half-sisters) ran the plantation while his father was away at war. During that time, Wesley fell in love with a slave girl named America. He often told the story of how he paid $100 for the slave girl who became his wife. Wesley and America had 18 children. The youngest, Emma, was my great-great-grandmother.

Times changed on the plantation as Wesley's half-sisters chose white Southern rebels as husbands. Rather than have Wesley subjected to ill treatment, his father arranged for Wesley and his family to move to a more liberal northern city, Quincy, Illinois. At the time Emma was only 8 years old.

Emma grew up in Quincy and she married Jack Bryant. They moved to Omaha, Nebraska at the turn of the century and had nine children. Their oldest child, Thurston, my great-grandfather, married a woman named May. This marriage produced six boys. Their second son, Marcy, was

Roots

my grandfather. Marcy Bryant married Mildred Penny from Nicodemus, Kansas.

Marcy and Mildred had four children and their third child, Doyle Harvey Bryant, is my father. I'm proud of my family heritage; the same as the Kennedy's, Rockefellers, Bushes or any of the Mayflower descendents. Is pride synonymous with arrogance, vanity, self-righteousness, over-confidence, conceit or egotism? I don't think so; I don't believe there is anything wrong with having a positive perception of yourself, your family, your community or your successes.

> *"I'm blessed to be standing on the shoulders of giants and I owe it to them to share our legacy."*
>
> *- Paul Bryant*

Why should I write this book? For the same reason I defend Omaha... It's about my family, my home and my community. These stories are the experiences that shaped and molded my life. I am nothing more than a link in the chain, an extension of those who came before me.

Nikki (Gabriel Union) and the fam...

Another generation
of Bryants...

Mom, Dad and
big brother...

Chapter Two

Motivation or Inspiration

What is the driving force behind a worthy goal or aspiration?

Do you remember what you were doing on September 11, 2001?

Many people remember exactly where they were when they heard the news of the assassinations of President John F. Kennedy in 1963 and civil rights leader Rev. Martin Luther King Jr. in 1968. They also remember astronaut Neil Armstrong's first step on the Moon in 1969, *"That's one small step for a man, one giant leap for mankind."* Those events were so monumental people remember exactly what they were doing at the precise time they heard the news.

13

Motivation or Inspiration

An event does not have to be of national significance to be burned into the core of one's memory. For instance, I will never forget the day I felt the inspiration to begin writing this book. That memory is so clear it's as if it happened yesterday.

I was one of 11 passengers aboard a private jet returning to Omaha from Phoenix, Arizona. I spent several days at a retreat golfing and swimming with some of the most wealthy and successful people in the world.

Gazing out the window as the aircraft ascended I watched the earth get smaller. Admiring the cherry wood cabinets and the full body leather seats, my thoughts submerged to an introspective area within my subconscious, *"How many people see the world from this angle, in this type of luxury?"* I wondered how a young black man such as myself – who grew up armed with nothing more than a pocketful of ambition – experienced so much.

14

Motivation or Inspiration

I had worked in corporate America for over twenty years and was successful in achieving my college goals of earning a Vice President title and a six-figure salary. I'd made loans as a banker, traveled internationally and dined with heads of state. An achiever on the rise, I was moving up the corporate ladder and had many of the outward trappings of success. I felt no need to apologize for being successful; my striving for excellence was at no one's expense. My outlook on life was simple; I desired the best. I enjoyed flying in first-class, eating fine foods, staying in premium hotels and conversing with intelligent people. I was doing all right for a poor boy from North Omaha.

However, underneath the, *"I-got-it-goin-on"* façade was an empty man. The recognition and experiences were great, but life had little meaning. My journey had turned into an endless pursuit of material wealth. My ultimate ambition was to attain money, prestige, power, and notoriety. My family, friends and loved ones were discounted, as I strived to climb the ladder of success. I had dedicated my

Motivation or Inspiration

life to a career, wasting energy, intellect and talent pursuing fruitless goals that once achieved were not rewarding. The quest for success had me living an unfulfilled life chasing a mirage of happiness.

I thought about the people who reach the pinnacle of success then succumb to the allure of drugs, alcohol or infidelity; these are the celebrities who appear to have all the fame and fortune, but their lives are out of control.

For some unexplainable reason, I felt compelled to write. I pulled out a pen and stationary and began to note down various events in my life, the good, the bad, the funny, and the sad. I knew my behavior was anti-social, but I couldn't help it. I buried my head in a notebook and didn't talk or interact with anyone. Putting the pen to paper became spiritual. The clarity of thought was so lucid; it appeared I was reliving each occurrence. I composed events that ran the spectrum from presentations on Capital Hill with United State Senators, to dark alley deals with gun toting drug dealers.

16

Motivation or Inspiration

The more I wrote, the deeper my understanding of life became. Leadership surfaced as a consistent theme in my writing. From my selection to the Student Council in second grade, to my promotion as Vice President for The Gallup Organization, to my current position of Executive Director for the Wesley House Leadership Academy, I viewed life through a leadership lens.

When the plane made its descent I raised my eyes from the paper and realized I had composed a series of vignettes that woven together created the fabric of my life. Through the years I've attempted to tie those stories together into a book, but I never seemed able to bring closure to the project.

My desire to finish this book intensified during the historic campaign between John McCain and Barack Obama. I had great empathy for Barack; our lives shared numerous correlations. We are both educated, professional, African American males around the same age. We are both married

17

with young families, and we have both been recognized for delivering an eloquent speech. Through first hand experience, I identified with his position of sticking to the high road while being the object of personal attacks during his campaign. I once made an attempt for a public office and know full well the sting of political arrows. Watching Barack Obama successfully navigate the political mine fields inspired me to quit procrastinating, step up my game and complete this book.

Another date forever burned into my memory is November 4, 2008; the day Barack Obama became the 44th President of the United States of America.

My family was at the home of a couple we have known for over 20 years. They invited several friends and relatives over to watch the election returns and the Bryant's were posted up on the sofa in front of the big screen television.

There was an eclectic mixture in the room; the man of the house was a faithful Republican and a career

18

Motivation or Inspiration

military man. He was proud to tow the party line, which led to many intense and spirited debates concerning the quality of leadership in government. For the past eight years he held the trump card because his guy was in office.

Tonight however, the Obama supporters were in the majority and we were feeling pretty good. We sensed this would be our night to celebrate. We were active viewers of the returns adding lively commentary to every pundit's remark. We wore t-shirts, hats and pins in anticipation of America electing its first black President. As the night wore on, it became obvious there were others in the room not supporting Obama; their stoic and non-communicative demeanor easily identified them. It was as if they were attending a funeral while everyone else was having a party.

This was a long, tough contest, and it brought out the best in our country. When the election was officially called, both candidates delivered their greatest speeches. We witnessed two leaders; one

Motivation or Inspiration

victorious and the other in defeat exhibit both class and dignity. No matter what side of the election you were on, you had to be proud of our system of democracy. The chest of everyone in the room, Republicans, Democrats and Independents was swelled with pride.

I know it's difficult for many people to understand why it took this election to give African Americans such a deep feeling of ownership in their country. America is a place where many blacks have prospered and have lived for several generations.

What these people must understand is African American history contains 300 plus years of slavery, and 100 years of Jim Crow segregation. Our ancestors endured the brutality of lynching, police dogs, water hoses, and bombings. Organizations like the KKK, Arian Nation and Skin Heads exist for the sole purpose of holding us back.

Why are we so happy? A civil rights movement was necessary just for us to obtain the right to vote!

Motivation or Inspiration

It was liberating for our souls to hear the majority of Americans say, *"We are willing to judge you by the content of your character and not the color of your skin."* For the very first time, I could tell my children, *"You can become anything in this country that you want,"* and I would believe it myself.

More tears were shed November 4th, than in any other Presidential election in history. My emotions were visible; I didn't know it was possible to have such feelings over a political election. I shed tears of joy finally knowing beyond a shadow of a doubt the sacrifices of my ancestors were not in vain. My children and the unborn generations of my family were full citizens of this country. We had a stake in America! This was my home and my country; I felt 100% American and proud of it! Many African Americans could finally identify with the pride exhibited by the martyr of the American Revolution, Nathan Hale, when he said, *"I regret that I have but one life to lose for my country."*

Motivation or Inspiration

The outpouring of emotions witnessed around the world was a global sigh of relief. America, the greatest country on the face of the earth, the symbol to those looking for justice and equality was once again focusing on the credo that *"All men are created equal regardless of race, creed, and religion or national origin."* People in foreign countries were just as excited as the Bryant family about Obama's victory. I was so inspired by the campaign and the world's response to Barack Obama, that I decided it was finally time to finish this book.

> *"Inspiration without motivation will often lead to procrastination."*   *- Paul E. Bryant*

This unfinished project was a constant reminder to me of incomplete business and it was a source of contention for my wife. I have been writing on and off for years. I thought it was done a couple of times, but releasing it never felt quite right. I now felt motivated to bring this book to a conclusion.

Motivation or Inspiration

Never before had the world been so focused on leadership. It seemed the stars aligned and directed me toward writing about Purpose Living Leadership.

Flying the friendly skies with Admiral Mies and Tim Santos

The Knights of Aksarben has
attracted Nebraska's Civic and
Business Leaders since 1895...

Chapter Three

Leadership

Are you Purpose or Profit Driven?

This book is about **Purpose Living Leadership**; the type of headship fondly remembered after it is gone. The focus will be on qualities worthy of reverence and exaltation. A large majority of Americans have opened their eyes and many people have become extremely dissatisfied with the quality of leadership in business and government. Far too many leaders seem more interested in personal gain than the plight of the people. My internal compass says there will never be another time like the present.

On my weekly radio program, Inside Urban America, I was a vocal critic of President Bush's decision to launch an unprovoked war with Iraq. That criticism most likely led to the cancellation of my show after 5 years on the air. Condemnation of

26

Leadership

Bush's foreign policy now seems justified, as the majority of Americans want to withdraw our troops from Iraq and President Bush suffers from the lowest approval ratings of any president in history.

How can the student learn if he has no teacher? I have been 'the First' or 'the Only' African American in more situations than I can remember. I was the only African American radio talk show host in the state of Nebraska; the first Black Business Development Officer for the 150-year-old First National Bank of Omaha, the first Black Male elected to my High School Hall of Fame, and the first Black Vice President for the 70+ year-old Gallup Organization. I believe there was purpose in every one of those circumstances. I felt like a pioneer leading the way, blazing a trail for a more talented, technologically savvy generation to follow. Similar to the experiences Jackie Robinson encountered in Baseball, the first African Americans in corporate offices had many obstacles to overcome. My survival required me to be a quick study.

I was the first person in my family to graduate from college. No one in my family held a professional job. It was a necessity for me to observe others to learn the nuances of leadership in corporate America. The work place is full of land mines waiting to derail the career of an unsuspecting employee. For many minorities it's like the commercial says, *"You never get a second chance to make a first impression."* We are the last hired and the first fired. My ascension up the corporate ladder was successful because I learned, then cloned the traits of successful leaders. I studied them closely, discovered what worked for me and then added my flavor to it. The final result was a crisp, upwardly mobile, corporate persona that took me from the back streets to boardrooms.

Leadership development is not a curriculum readily offered to youth in inner cities. Traditional

Leadership

programs like the Boy Scouts have a strong leadership component but they lack appeal to urban youth. In order for the next generation to adequately carry the baton of leadership, they need to know what's expected of them. And in order for them to successfully lead their children to the next level, they need to know how to get there themselves. My goal is to provide a roadmap for Urban Youth to successfully navigate mainstream America.

When the student is ready the teacher will appear. In banking there is a term called the four C's of credit. Its premise is that every bankable deal consists of four elements: Capital, Collateral, Capacity and Character. A lender can determine with a high degree of certainty a borrower's ability to repay a loan based on the four C's of credit. CAPITAL: A borrower must be able to put some of their money into the deal. COLLATERAL: The borrower must pledge security for the loan to guarantee the lender will get repaid. CAPACITY: The borrower must have an existing source of

29

revenues; they must demonstrate the ability to repay new debt and satisfy existing obligations. The fourth C; CHARACTER, is the most important and it's the most difficult to define. Webster's Dictionary describes character as: *"The aggregate of features and traits that form the individual nature of some person or thing."* What???

Most people would agree that character is an important trait for selecting a partner in marriage or in business. But for some reason, until this last presidential election, we overlooked character when it came to selecting our leaders. Character became a missing element in 21st century leadership.

The pursuit of personal satisfaction is eroding the moral fiber of humanity. Greed has become the motivation for far too many of us. Horrendous decisions are made based on a simple premise that nothing is more important than the accumulation of wealth and power. Our society is content playing 'follow the leader' with people driven by self-

Leadership

interest. The quest for money and control has our culture sliding down a slippery slope. Self-destruction is what we will find at the bottom of the hill.

We only need to peel away the outer layer of the onion to find the residue of following misguided leadership... We live in a time when the Religious, Business and Political leaders cannot be trusted. The Church protects pedophiles; Corporate Executives embezzle funds, lay off thousands of workers and retire with million dollar pensions. Perceptions of dishonest, sleazy and untrustworthy politicians are becoming the norm rather than the exception. All you have to do is read the newspaper or watch television to clearly see that bad news rules the day. Much too often the crisis at hand is the result of a self-serving decision made by someone in authority. The lack of leadership will lead to the downfall of America. History will confirm great civilizations do not fall from being conquered by external forces. They implode under

Leadership

the weight of misguided decisions made by a series of pathetic leaders. All the great Dynasties, Assyria, Israel, Babylon, Persia, Egypt, Rome and Greece all collapsed from within.

To be labeled a leader in today's society, you only need a large sum of money. It doesn't matter how your wealth was acquired; inheritance, hard work, or illegal behavior. He who has the resources is deemed successful. The media will freely broadcast your image and ideas into millions of homes, thus equipping you with everything necessary to influence the masses. Hence we have the unanswerable question, "what comes first, the money or the media."

Don't get me wrong; I don't loathe rich people. If my life goes according to plan, I will be a member of the club. However, I believe its one thing to have wealth and quite another to let your wealth have you. A superficial life awaits the person only known for what they own.

32

Leadership

What happened to the leadership of yesteryear? Back in the good old days when we had leaders we could count on, leaders we could trust. There is a paradox between **Purpose Living Leaders** who pursue a higher calling and **Profit Driven Leaders** who pursue financial gain and personal recognition.

Purpose Living Leaders challenge us to reach for a higher standard. Remember when there were leaders worthy of our respect and adulation because they stood for something? John F. Kennedy, Martin Luther King Jr. and Nelson Mandela encouraged us to reach deep within ourselves to find greatness as did Mother Teresa and Mahatma Ghandi. There were also sports heroes of yesterday who won the hearts and minds of people across America like Muhammad Ali, Babe Ruth, Vince Lombardi, Arthur Ashe; Jackie Robinson and Gale Sayers. They overcame obstacles, reached the pinnacle of success and inspired us to do, be, and become more. They were more concerned with fulfilling their purpose than filling their pockets. These altruistic

33

Leadership

Legacy Leaving Leaders stood out, because they stood up.

Profit Driven Leaders however, could care less about your needs or what you are reaching for, as long as they are getting paid. They are cut from a different cloth. It doesn't matter if they are global, national or local; they are motivated by greed. This lack of character gives them an entitlement mindset and their decisions are based strictly on personal gain. In the twilight of their careers they have self-serving thoughts of achieving immortality and this is when they focus on creating their legacy. Unfortunately for them, the cast has been set and the dye poured; the sum of their choices will determine how they will be remembered. In my opinion, Vice President Dick Chaney and Illinois' Governor Rod Blagojevich are the epitome of Profit Driven Leaders.

Profit Driven Leaders spend their lives in the proverbial rat race, full participants in the futile chase for material wealth. They follow clever mantra's like, "He who dies with the most toys, wins." When actually, he who dies with the most toys, dies! The winner is the one whose positive influence is felt long after they are gone; the Legacy Leaving Leader.

The people who make a difference are not the ones with the most credentials, the most money or the most awards. We can all name a teacher who aided in our journey through school. Everybody has someone who has helped them make it through a difficult time. It's easy to name the people who have taught us something worthwhile or who have made us feel appreciated and special. The people who impact our lives are the ones who care. No one remembers the headliners of yesterday; do you?

- Name the last five Super Bowl winners?
- Name the last five World Series winners?

35

Leadership

- Name the last five Heisman trophy winners?
- Name five winners of the Nobel Peace Prize?
- Name the five wealthiest people in the world?
- Name five winners of the Miss America pageant?
- Name five people who have won the Pulitzer Prize?
- Name the last five Academy Award winners for best actor or actress?

These are no second-rate achievers. They are the best in their fields, but eventually the applause dies, awards tarnish, achievements are forgotten and certificates are buried with their owners. To paraphrase the bible, *"What profit is it for a man to gain the world if he loses his soul?"*

Purpose Living Leaders do not seek glory; they actively work to complete the task at which they

36

Leadership

were put on this earth to accomplish. They know true happiness is having Joy in their heart, Purpose in their step and Passion for what they do.

One of the major events in American History occurred when Barack Obama was sworn in as the 44th President of the United States. Over two million people endured freezing temperatures to witness the inaugural ceremony of the first African American Commander in Chief. This was the world's largest most diverse crowd in history.

Modern history has not seen a leader assume the reigns of power with a more overwhelming mandate. Millions of Americans unified on one accord to wish the new president success.

My experience working with leaders covers the spectrum from Politics, Business, Sports, Religion and most notably Youth. I've witnessed great leaders successfully maneuver the worst of times and I've watched insignificant leaders muddle

37

Leadership

through the best of times. Watching the departure of the Bush administration raised these thoughts; *"Why is Barack so loved and why did George Bush have such a low approval rating?"*

I stayed up most of the night watching CNN and reflecting on the events of the day. I thought about Barack Obama, his awesome presence and the way he inspires people around the world. I thought about George Bush and Dick Chaney, and their uneventful exit. There were no tears, no crowds, no pomp and circumstance for their departure. The burning question in my mind was, *"What is it that distinguishes someone as a Purpose Living Leader?"*

Over the next few days I continued the methodical examination of those philosophical annotations. I discovered a consistent recurring pattern of thoughts, feelings and behaviors exhibited by leaders of substance. I assembled those traits into a

Leadership

formula known as, **The Equation for Purpose Living Leadership.**

$$(VP + CP) \div (F \times H) = I$$

Vision   Courage
* &   +   &   ÷   Faith x Hope = Influence*
Purpose   Perseverance

A Purpose Living Leader has a **Vision** for where they want to go and an altruistic **Purpose** for reaching that destination. **Courage** is a must for the Purpose Living Leader because pursuing their vision will often take them to the road less traveled. **Perseverance** is what they need to stay the course when the road gets rough and opposition surfaces. **Faith** is an unwavering belief that they will succeed no matter what the obstacles and it empowers them to persist without quitting. **Hope** is future focused faith; to look forward with unwavering optimism. And **Influence** is the most important element of leadership. Without followers a leader will find it difficult to reach their destination. Make no

39

mistake about it; Leaders with the DNA of a Purpose Living Leader have impact! Their Legacies are remembered long after they are gone.

Take a moment and think of the monumental experiences in your life. Capture the memories as they leap forward in your mind. Does a pattern emerge? The experiences of your past will guide you toward your purpose. As I look over my life there is a history of involvement; a clearly identifiable track record of working to improve the lives of children.

Experiences build knowledge, and over time accumulated knowledge will turn into wisdom. Wisdom is the foundation of understanding, and understanding is the *'IT'* factor Purpose Living Leaders use to impact the world!

"A temporary setback is sometimes the price you pay for going against the grain; it's the cost of being a leader."
                                                                    –Paul Bryant

Chapter Four

Vision

A dream or a vision; what's the difference?

All Purpose Living Leaders have vision. They have an image in their head of how things are supposed to be. This illustration is so clear they can see its impact on others. The picture is so perfect that the leader dreams about its fruition.

There is a major difference however, between a dream and a vision. After a dream you wake up and continue with your day. A vision stays with you and it doesn't go away. You continue to see and think about the images in your mind both day and night. Life will start presenting you with choices, daily decisions that lead you closer to that vision.

There is no way to predict how or when a vision will come. Sometimes they appear in a dream and

41

Vision

then there are times when they are the result of an extraordinary experience. The things you dream about find a way into your consciousness. The following story is about a vision I had as a young boy that came to fruition.

I was 14 years old and had just won the MVP trophy at the honors banquet for my football team. Winning the Ricky Smith Memorial Trophy allowed me to savor the sweet taste of success. I thoroughly enjoyed being the man of the moment and made a mental note to not let that experience be the last time I was in front of an audience.

The year was 1972; the University of Nebraska Cornhuskers had won the National Collegiate Football Championship and Johnny Rogers had won the Heisman Trophy. Football was at an all time high in Nebraska, but the Huskers were not the team of the hour.

Vision

This was the end of season banquet for the Schweizer's midget league football team. We had an undefeated season but suffered a nail biting loss in the championship game. That loss however, was not a damper on the end of season celebration. All the individual trophies had been awarded and it was now time to recognize the winner of the MVP Trophy. The air was thick with anxiety and every boy in the room was hoping to win. I looked to my left and noticed one of my friends had his fingers crossed, and then I looked to my right and another friend was praying.

All nervousness ended when the emcee said, *"This year's winner of the Ricky Smith Memorial Trophy is... Paul Br-r-r-yant!"* Something happened when I heard my name called over the microphone. All eyes searched the room to find the person who warranted individual recognition. As I rose from my chair to walk to the front, time slowed down. Every step was deliberate. I could feel everyone in the room looking at me. In their eyes I saw support,

43

Vision

pride, excitement and envy. The sound of applause was music to my ears. This was my 15 minutes of fame and I wanted to savor every minute of it. I looked success in the eye and she winked back; it was love at first sight.

I reached the podium and found myself face-to-face with the legendary running back for the Chicago Bears, Gale Sayers, the youngest person admitted to the NFL Hall of Fame! This was the man who scored 6 touchdowns in one game; the author of the book, *I am Third* and the inspiration for the movie Brian's Song. Every kid in the room wanted to shake Gale's hand and he was standing at the podium waiting to shake mine. Also waiting at the head table was the All American, Olympic Gold medalist and NBA World Champion, Bob Boozer. My head was in the clouds and the rest of that evening was a blur. Days later when I would review the event in my mind, what I remembered most was being on stage.

Vision

The next morning my picture with Gale Sayers was in the newspaper. At school I was met with excitement from my classmates and received congratulations from many of the teachers. This was about as much success as an eighth grade boy could handle. I felt a connection with Gale Sayers. I knew he made hundreds of presentations and signed thousands of autographs but for some reason I felt a relationship. I knew our lives were destined to intersect at some point in the future. I made a vow to be successful, to live a life that would allow me the opportunity to once again share the podium with Gale Sayers.

It was around that time I began to dream of being in front of audiences; not as an award recipient, but as the Master of Ceremonies. I envisioned myself in public speaking situations, as a preacher, a news reporter or a politician. I constantly critiqued actors and comedians, comparing how I would have done or said something differently. I didn't know how to

Vision

get there, but I wanted the microphone; I wanted to be on stage.

With proper guidance in college I might have majored in speech or communications. Looking back and taking an inventory of my life, I can see that God has blessed me with exactly what I dreamed of doing. I currently speak well over 100 times a year. I've spoken to both national and international audiences and have hosted television and radio programs. But one of by biggest thrills is the creation of the Gale Sayers Golf Classic. In the past four years over a quarter of a million dollars has been raised for my youth program through events that feature Gale's name. My son has even had the pleasure of introducing Gale at our annual dinner.

It's been said that a vision is a mental picture of a goal or aspiration, a revelation of a future destination that's waiting for us to come forward and stake our claim. I believe that a vision is

46

Vision

God's way of allowing us to see mile markers on the road to our destiny.

My vision still involves a stage, but the purpose is more defined. I see myself using my talents to inspire young people to overcome obstacles, persevere hardships and reach for their God given potential.

I feel strongly about working with young people because they are vulnerable. These are perilous times and our society is being overrun with a self-centered; it's all about me mentality. Popular culture says looking out for number one is an essential element of attaining success. Legions of young people believe the pursuit of pleasure is life's ultimate achievement. Their unbridled desire for gratification has produced growing numbers of sexually transmitted diseases, unmarried pregnancies and a record number of juveniles matriculating through the criminal justice system. Students arming themselves and shooting

47

Vision

classmates is a serious concern for every school in America. Historic numbers of children are committing suicide.

Nowhere in America is the residue of our culture more prevalent than within the African American community. Recipients of the worst of society's ills, African Americans are 12% of the population, 30% of the poor, 44% of all prisoners. A shocking 67% of African American children are born out of wedlock.

By virtually any measure – education, economics, employment or health – the spirit of black America is being stripped away. By the 4th grade 69% of black children cannot read at grade level compared to 29% among white children; 45% of black children live below the poverty line compared to 16% of white children.

Blacks account for only 13% of drug users but 35% of all drug possession arrests and 74% of those sentenced to prison for drug possession. And when

Vision

the microscope is held over African American males, the statistics become even more striking. The chances of going to prison are 32.2% for black males, 17.4 % for Hispanic males and 5.9% for white males. More black men earn their high school equivalency diplomas in prison each year than graduate from college. Over 1.46 million black men have lost their right to vote due to felony convictions.

The homicide rate for black males is seven times the rate for white males. The Justice Department estimates that one out of every 21 black men can expect to be murdered. Black men are nine times as likely as white men to die from AIDS and life expectancy for black men is 69.2 years – more than six years shorter than that of white men.

Only 41% of black male students graduate from high school in America. At comparable educational levels, black men earn 67% of what white men make. A white male with a high school diploma is

Vision

just as likely to have a job and tends to earn just as much as a black male with a college degree.

With marginal success in education and limited access to the economic mainstream, the future for Black children is depressing. Single parent families, racism, terrible schools and a subculture that glorifies swagger over work all contribute to the desolation of black communities across America. Too many children grow up fatherless without positive role models. They have no examples to show them how to successfully navigate the mainstream of society.

I love my culture and see no worthier calling than to dedicate my career toward changing these statistics. I envision a day when African American children look forward to achieving in their academics as much as they look forward to achieving in athletics; and when parents appreciate intellectual accomplishments as much as physical activities. I believe it was President John Kennedy who said,

Vision

"Some men see things as they are and say, Why? I dream of things that never were and say, Why not!"

What do you see? Is there some thought or idea that stays with you day and night? Don't dismiss it, it just might be your destiny saying, *"Come and get me..."*

"Vision is a recurring mental picture that continues to find its way into the minds eye. It's a clear, vivid, snapshot of an event yet to happen. It's the ability to see into the future."   *- Paul Bryant*

DejaVu!

The retirement
of Gale' Sayers
Central High
Jersey

Bryant, Sayers . . . Trophy for young grid star.

Sayers' Quickness Holds Up,
So 1972 Grid Hopes Bloom

Chapter Five

Purpose

Are you doing what you do best?

Without Purpose it's impossible to be a Purpose Living Leader. PLL's believe their actions make a significant contribution to the better good. They are empowered by the connection between their actions and some altruistic objective. When a leader focuses their talents, skills, and abilities on a vision it's captivating. Their dedication draws people toward their cause.

There's something magical about finding that mission you were placed on this earth to accomplish. When your calling becomes clear, the stars align and you are empowered with the tenacity to triumph over problems. You develop a single mindedness; a synergy of thought and action that provides clarity of intention and the drive to

53

Purpose

succeed. The experiences encountered while actively pursuing a vision will validate your purpose.

My purpose is to challenge and inspire people to persevere through adversity to achieve greatness. I believe this is the reason for which God allowed me to come into this world. Two specific events caused me to leave a 20-year career in corporate America and revive a non-profit agency on the verge of bankruptcy.

The first happened one spring afternoon when a group of sixth grade students were determined to give me the substitute teacher welcome reception.

During the spring of 2002 I volunteered with the Urban League as a presenter in the BEEP (Black Executive Exchange Program) to speak to a class at an inner city elementary school. I could not believe the treatment I received from the students after my introduction. Slumping in their seats with an 'I

Purpose

don't care' attitude they challenged me for control of the class. Their resistance was so stanch and their dissent so uniform; it was obvious to me they were not impressed. I could not believe their demeanor or the tone in which they addressed me.

To my chagrin, their teacher sat quietly in the back of the room. I didn't know if she wanted to observe how a black man would deal with a room full of unruly black kids or was she simply relieved not to be the object of their contempt for a few moments.

It seemed improbable that any child could learn in that environment. One thing was certain; my presentation was going down hill fast and a quick decisive action was required if I ever planned to gain the attention and respect of those students.

I shut the door, took off my jacket, loosened my tie and ever so slowly rolled up my sleeves. And then I came with it… I chastised those kids like they were mine… It was on. *"How dare you disrespect me, I*

Purpose

don't know who you think I am, but you're about to find out!" Oh yes, I went there... And I stayed there... *"I'm the baddest one in this class, anyone who feels different, stand up!"*

I must have gotten loud because the principal walked in the room. I wasn't deterred, I continued with the verbal assault. *"If you were my children, I'd whip your butts for acting this way in school!"* The principal, like the teacher, moved to the back of the room, sat quietly and didn't utter a word. All of my buttons were pushed; *"Up in here acting like a bunch of fools, nobody should have to put up with this crap...You can't be more than 10 years old, how dare you disrespect me!"*

For about an hour I demanded and received their attention. Sharing many of my personal experiences to let them know they didn't have a monopoly on misery. Never before had I so openly discussed my background. When I finished, much of my life was

Purpose

laying on the floor. Drained and depressed I couldn't wait to get out of that school.

Just as I was leaving the building three of the toughest kids in the class came running up to me. *"Mr. Bryant, are you going to come back?"* They actually had the nerve to ask if I would come speak to them again! My lips said, *'yes'* but my mind said, *"HELL NO!"* I never wanted to see the inside of that school or the faces of those students again.

The following week I couldn't stop thinking about those rowdy kids and how easily they caused me to loose my composure. I was still angry with them. I called the school and scheduled a meeting with the principal. I needed to share my observations with her and I also wanted to give that class another piece of my mind. After our talk the principal handed me a large envelope and said, *"Thank you for coming Mr. Bryant, you saved me postage."* To my surprise, several of the students had written letters to me. I was flabbergasted! What did that

Purpose

group of ruffians have to say? As soon as I reached the parking lot I ripped open the envelope and began to read their letters. I sat in my car and read them all. As I read the tears rolled down my face...

Dear Bryant,

Are you going to come back to our class this year? I really enjoyed what you said, and how you told us to listen. You know I have not gotten in trouble since I have been listening, following directions and staying out of trouble on the streets. I was in a crew called R,T,K,C, until you came and talk to us. I want you to come back, so I won't get in trouble. This is some things we did; we stole stuff from stores, jump people, and fought a lot, stayed out late, and did bad things. I can change my behavior by getting out the crew like I did. When I have free time I won't go to them I will study to reach a goal.

Sincerely
Andre

P.S. I hope you come back soon

Purpose

Dear Mr. Bryant,

I enjoyed you bring in my classroom. Please come back. Your words, I think help me see life in a different way. I think I am a better person because of you. After you told your story, I know that I should look to my dreams. I should not care what people think of me. You also showed me that I should stand up for my rights. I hope you come back to my classroom and share some more with me and my classmates. I know that one day I will be successful as you are. Your children should be proud of you. They should grow up to be just like you. Let God bless your soul.

Sincerely,
Marie

Dear Mr. Bryant,

Will you come back to our class and just speak of what you know. When Andre Mills came in he bored me to death and he sent

Purpose

the girls out of the room for a long time. I hope you come back to talk.

If you come back we will probably be more friendly because we know you. You treat everyone like you treat your kids. Everybody knows and understands what you're talking about. They know you listen to everybody too.

I have a lot of things I want to be when I grow up. I could have brought my video camera but I didn't have any film. Can you please come back?

Sincerely,
Nadia

Dear Mr. Bryant,

I was wandering how it was going to collage for a degree.

I was just asking because I want to be the first person in my family to go to collage. Let me tell you a little bit about myself, my name is Stephany, I will be 12 in November 21, 1990. I have 5 siblings, 3 older and 2

Purpose

---

younger (I'm stuck in the middle!) I need some advice, about school and home. You may be able to help me with, O.K. ready how am I supposed to be smart, look out for my younger sisters, get my work done (on time) , behave and have time for my self and have time for my friends? PLEASE HELP ME

> *Sincerely,*
> *Stephany*

Dear Mr. Bryant,

Hi my name is Shan'e. I want to tell you about myself. I'm really smart. I have lots of talent. I'm good in Spelling. That is my favorite work to do in my class. The reason I like school so much is because I want to do some fun things in my life. I want to get an education and go to college. I hope you get my letter. Could you please come back to our classroom?

I liked hearing what you said. I'm really sorry what happened to your Dad. We

Purpose

---

really want you to come back to our classroom.

Sincerely,
Shan'e

Dear Mr. Bryant,

What you said was great. I am sorry for the people who were being rude and I am sorry about your dad. That made me feel sad.

I hope you can sale me some advice on how not to get a temper with others, how to follow directions, and how to work will with others. I am not bad at those three things. I just need to work on it.

I hope some other time you can back. Everybody wants you to come back. Write us all back, please! SEE YOU LATER! Bye!

Sincerely,
Anthony

Purpose

Dear Mr. Bryant,

I enjoyed your speech it was really good. For my education I will be a lawyer, judge, mayor. Then I want to be the first woman president and that is how I want to full- fill my dream.

Then I want to take care of my family and friends that need my help. I'm going to take my sister-in-law out of Tommy Rose apartments take care of my nephews, cousins and other family and friends. The reason why I'm telling you this because I have a bad life well not exactly bad I'm blessed be living with my aunty. I hope you come back and tell us more about your life.

Sincerely,
Rakeyia

From that day forward, I made a commitment to be real with young people. To openly share my life experiences with them, the good the bad, the funny and the sad. I spoke to that class once a month for

Purpose

the rest of the semester and the following year I presented the commencement address to the graduating class of eighth grade students.

I will never forget those students. I didn't know my words could touch lives. Because of them I found my purpose: *To inspire children to overcome obstacles and persevere hardships to seek the greatness God has placed within them.*

The second event to steer me toward my purpose occurred during the summer of 2005 when the course of my life took a dramatic change from success to significance. At the time, I worked with the Wells Fargo Bank as a business banker. My job was to build relationships with key clientele. I managed a $75,000,000 portfolio and worked in an upscale area of the community called Regency.

One morning two of my colleagues were having a discussion outside of my office about a business that recently applied for a loan. I overheard one of

Purpose

them say, "There is no way in HELL I'd lend them money! They will be out of business in three months." The other one chuckled and said, "They must think we're a fricken charity." The wheels of destiny started in motion the moment I stepped out of my office to butt-in on their conversation.

The company whose demise they were so casually discussing was the Wesley House, a 135-year-old social service organization located in North Omaha, the heart of the African American community. The Wesley House was once a prominent organization with a rich history of developing programs that grew into self-supporting businesses. I hated the thought of another African American managed business closing under a cloud of mismanagement. I was saddened to discover the Wesley House was the topic of discussion.

I asked for the financials to see if there was anything I could do for the agency, to make sure every avenue had been explored. There's an old

65

saying in banking, "You can find 99 reasons to turn a loan down, but a good loan officer will find the 1 reason to make a loan."

As I read through the file that evening it became apparent The Wesley House was a total disaster. It was a textbook case for what happens to a mismanaged business. Two years prior (2003) the United Way stopped funding them; TWO HUNDRED and EIGHTY THOUSAND dollars out of their annual budget! Approximately two years later the administration depleted a $500,000 reserve. In December of 2004 the Executive Director resigned; in February and March of 2005 the board cancelled all programs and released the entire staff. It was April and they were shopping banks looking for a loan to cover expenses. Ray Charles could see this was not a bankable deal...

The next morning I called their board chairman and asked if they had an alternative strategy because they would not be able to secure financing. He told

Purpose

me they were currently searching for an Executive Director. The board felt the right leadership would be able to turn things around. I wished him well, hung up the phone and said aloud, *"No leader worth his salt will take that job."*

At home that evening all I could think about was the Wesley House. I couldn't get them out of my head. Another North Omaha based business was going to close under a cloud of incompetence. Before going to sleep, I prayed to God and asked if there was anything I could do to help.

The next morning I woke at 3:00am and for some unexplainable reason got out of bed, went downstairs and picked up the bible. I wasn't looking for a particular chapter or verse; by random selection I opened it to the book of Nehemiah and began reading the amazing story of a faithful man called by God for a special mission. He lived during the Israelites second period of captivity and worked as the cupbearer for Artaxerxes, King of

Persia. Because of his position Nehemiah heard many things that were meant for the kings ears only.

He overheard a report on the project to rebuild Jerusalem that was not good. Seventy years earlier a number of Jews had been released so they could rebuild the holy city and the work was incomplete. King Artaxerxes was at a crossroads as to whether he should continue to support the effort. Nehemiah felt pricked in his heart to do something. He felt compelled to leave his job to go rebuild the wall. Because of his faith, God touched King Artaxerxes heart and not only was Nehemiah granted his freedom, but he won the support of the people and finished rebuilding the wall in 52 days.

The correlations between rebuilding the Wall and rebuilding the Wesley house, leaving a good job with a king and leaving a good job with a bank were uncanny. I sat there on my sofa at 3:30am and thought, "Is GOD speaking to me?" The hair on the back of my neck was standing up straight. Did God

Purpose

want me to revive the Wesley House? I thought, "How does GOD speak to us in 2005?" He could set a bush aflame and a voice from nowhere could issue instructions. He is GOD, he's done it before and he is totally capable of doing it again. The thought of GOD, the ultimate CEO, communicating with me was overwhelming.

The truth of the matter is that I prayed in earnest asking what I could do to help the Wesley House. And God woke me and led me to his word. The ball was now in my court. I surmised he wanted me to accept the challenge of rebuilding and preserving the history of a 135-year-old historic organization. Even though the toilet was flushed and the Wesley House was circling around in the bowl, with his help I could stop it from going down the drain.

The next morning I called the Wesley House Chairman and started lobbying for the job. I felt drawn to the position. A persistent voice in my head urged me to apply; Oprah Winfrey calls this

Purpose

voice a God Whisper. I was convinced that going for the Wesley House job was something I was supposed to do. I officially tossed my hat in the ring and three weeks later was offered the position.

Many of my friends, former clients and business associates thought I was going through a mid life crisis. By societal standards I had it made, a great job, making big bucks, and an office in a prestigious location. I knew behind their smiles and nods of approval they thought I was crazy.

Their opinions didn't matter because I was pursuing my purpose with passion. To anyone who asked, *"Why did you leave the bank?"* I told the story of waking at 3am and reading Nehemiah with righteous indignation. My trek to purpose was a story I shared freely.

I was unfulfilled; I had talents and abilities not being utilized. I felt my life's effort had to consist of more than just impacting the bottom line for a

Purpose

company. The position at the Wesley House was a leap backwards in terms of status and income. Not only would I make less money, but also I would have to leave my office in the suburbs for a store front in the hood. My clients would no longer be affluent businessmen. The corporate executive brand I had built over the last 20 years would be obliterated. It didn't bother me however; I was unfazed because I had found my purpose.

My bubble burst two days before my start date when the chairman invited me to lunch and informed me the Wesley House was Forty Thousand dollars in debt! Bright red stop signs flashed before my eyes. How was I supposed to lead an agency with out a staff, no programs and a forty thousand dollar deficit? The organization already had a cloud of ineptness over its head from the United Way pulling its funding. I didn't have an 'S' on my chest; I wasn't Superman. A forty thousand dollar shortfall was more than I bargained for.

Purpose

I lost my appetite and a whirlwind of thoughts ran through my mind. Was this board dishonest or just incompetent? This $40,000 obligation was not on the financials they presented to the bank. What other surprises did they have? Not only was I taking my family for a ride on a financial rollercoaster, but also my first assignment would now be to pull the organization out of an economic hole.

I didn't know if I still wanted the job. I left the meeting with serious reservations; depression is the only way to describe my mental state of mind. How could I tell my wife, Robin, that I was leaving Wells Fargo to lead an organization that was $40,000 in the hole? For two weeks I had been boasting about finding purpose, waking at 3:00am, reading Nehemiah, following my inner voice. My wife never questioned my decision, even though I knew she had concerns. We were in the beginning stages of building our first home. When I shared my

Purpose

decision to make a career move, her only question was, *"Will this affect our plans to build a new house?"* My immediate response was *"Absolutely not"* and her worries were eliminated.

I didn't know how to break the news to her, so I didn't. I avoided speaking with Robin that evening and made it to bed without sharing the news. I prayed before getting into bed and asked GOD for solutions. *"Dear God, were you really speaking to me, did you really want me to take this position?"*

As I lay in bed, all I could think about was the debt and what Robin's response would be when I told her. The number forty thousand circled above my head like the proverbial sheep. I was in a dreamlike state between sleep and consciousness when suddenly the number forty began to take on biblical significance. I thought about Noah and the Arc and how it rained for 40 days and 40 nights. I thought about Moses and the Israelites and how they wandered around in the wilderness for 40 years. I thought about Jesus. After John baptized him he went to the wilderness fasted and was tempted by Satan for 40 days and after his resurrection he showed himself to his disciples for 40 days. I thought about King Saul, King David, and King Solomon, they all ruled 40 years.

I also thought about everyone in the bible whom God had given a task. They all faced a crossroads; weather to follow their faith or choose the path society said was more desirable. I decided to lean on my faith. GOD is the ultimate power in this universe and if he wanted me to take this job then he would make a way for me to succeed. I decided to choose the path less traveled and take the job. I also decided not to tell Robin about the debt...

My board of Directors planned a welcome reception at the end of my first day on the job. This was my first opportunity to meet with my twelve new bosses. After the introductions and a few pleasantries one of my board members decided to turn the party into a working meeting. She expressed her excitement with my acceptance of the position and felt we should waist no time informing the public. *"I'll write the press release, you call the television stations, and you contact the newspapers. Who has any connections with the radio stations?"* She wasn't an officer on the board; but she was definitely in control. She intercepted the ball and started sprinting toward the goal line. She was just about to dive in the end zone when another board member asked, *"Paul, do you have any suggestions on how you would like to announce your acceptance of this position."*

Personally, I preferred to enter the job quietly and gain a more thorough understanding of the organization. I wanted to get a few successes under my belt before subjecting myself to the scrutiny of the press. The room fell silent when I said, *"I'd rather roll up my sleeves and do some work before we make a public announcement."*

Purpose

I heard a faint tone in my head, it said, *"Eliminate the debt before seeking publicity. Trust me and this debt will be gone in forty days."* I knew that familiar accent. It was the same voice that woke me up at 3:00am. It was the same voice that reminded me of the significance of the number forty; I had to listen. Without hesitation, I spoke out and told the board I would raise $40,000 in 40 days! Their facial expressions spoke volumes. Here's this guy they just hired, his first day on the job, proposing he could eliminate forty thousand of debt without a major foundation, corporation or a large supporter in his corner.

I wrote a $100 personal check and passionately encouraged them to join me on a quest to raise forty thousand dollars. I thought my gesture would generate enthusiasm. Reality set in when not one board member matched my contribution. I thought, *"Lord, how will I raise this money?"* The voice in my head told me, *"Have faith."*

Purpose

The reluctance of my board members was understandable. They were season ticket holders to the Wesley House's demise and didn't want to experience another failure. It was during their watch the United Way pulled its funding and they were present as the past administration depleted half a million dollars of reserves. These were the people who had to make the difficult decision to cut programs and release the staff. As doubtful as they were however, not one of them stepped in the way of my vision.

I began speaking to every group, organization, association or business that would listen. Kiwanis, Rotary, Optimist and Lions Clubs; to my surprise, people started donating money after my presentations. Anonymous $10, $50 and $100 dollar checks started arriving in the mail.

I immediately saw the need to select a programmatic thrust. After every presentation someone would ask, *"What are your programs?*

Purpose

Who do you service?" These were valid questions for which I had no answer. It was extremely optimistic to assume I could raise forty thousand dollars without a program.

The Wesley House is geographically located in the heart of the African American community; any metric used to measure a healthy community; graduation rates, teen pregnancies; sexually transmitted disease, drugs, gang activity, crime and violence was an issue in our front yard.

Again, I asked GOD for direction and again he answered. I was led to create a Mecca for intellectual achievers. An Academy of Excellence focused on academics for children who wanted to reach their full potential. The Wesley House would be an oasis of hope on an island of despair, targeting children and families who wanted to improve their lives.

Purpose

Most youth service programs in the inner city are structured to service At Risk Youths, Juvenile Delinquents, Truants, Ex Offenders, Ex Gang Members, etc. These are great programs and they provide a fantastic service to a number of families, but none of them target the kids who like to read or the ones interested in technology. There was no place for a child to participate in debate or a spelling bee. Where could they learn to play chess or bridge?

The child who performs well in school is given a pat on the back and encouraged to keep up the good work; they are told their efforts will really pay off in the future. However, amongst their peers they are ridiculed and called names like Geeks and Nerds. Young Black achievers are called Uncle Toms and Sell Outs and are accused of trying to act white for getting good grades. They are social outcasts left to find the path to success on their own. Meanwhile a series of mentoring and diversion programs await the child who decides not to perform in school.

Purpose

Conventional wisdom says children who do well have it made and therefore don't need any help. But in reality, intelligent children are confronted with the same issues and challenges as any other child growing up poor in the inner city. The allure of urban culture attracts them all. The streets will recognize, recruit and redirect these young people if society does not. An achiever is valuable in the streets for the same reasons they are valuable in a corporation. The talents necessary to manage employees in a business are the same talents necessary to direct members of a street gang. The jails are full of smart people who made bad decisions. There are no limits to the influence of peer pressure. Children will take extreme measures just to fit in.

The more I spoke, the clearer the picture became; meaningful long-term progress would only occur through the identification and multiplication of talent. The Wesley House Leadership Academy was founded to nurture and develop the next

Purpose

generation of leaders. The best way to rebuild a community is to invest in its future leaders. Through family centered programming we promote *Excellence in Academic Achievement.* We teach children to understand, accumulate and retain wealth, empowering them for leadership in the workforce, community and their families. *"Smart People Win"* is the mantra we carry as we strive to create an environment where it is cool to be smart. My goal is to make acting "Presidential" the new cool for youth in urban America.

I challenge young people to break the cycle of poverty and not adopt an entitlement mindset. John Bryant, CEO of the Hope Center in Los Angeles says, *"There is a difference between being broke and being poor. Being broke is a temporary financial condition, but being poor is a debilitating mindset and a depressed condition of the spirit."* Everyday at the Wesley House Leadership Academy children are encouraged to NEVER – EVER be poor.

Purpose

With God's favor I raised forty thousand dollars in thirty-six days! And on my wife's birthday we spent our first night in our new home.

Our Next Generation of Leaders...

Wesley House Academy Students visit Ariel Academy

Mutual of Omaha Chairman
& CEO Daniel P. Neary

Annual Meeting
Wallace R. Weitz Company

Green Bay Packer Great
Paul Horning

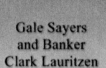

Gale Sayers
and Banker
Clark Lauritzen

Author, Michael Eric Dyson

Actor, Hill Harper

Entrepreneur, Stedman Graham

Chapter Six

Courage

When and where did you find it?

A Purpose Living Leader with vision, driven by purpose, must have the courage to act. Every leader will face opposition. Their success or failure will be determined by how they deal with conflict.

It has been said that someone with courage possesses the nerve to do what others will not. Descriptors for courage include words like bravery, heroism and valor. Are people born with courage, or are courageous deeds just a response to life's circumstances?

> *"Courage, the audacity to look fear in the face with enough backbone to move for ward."*
>
> *-Paul Bryant*

Courage

One of the most fearless and spontaneous acts in my life was a result of a chance encounter aboard a cruise ship. My wife and I were invited by Oprah Winfrey to celebrate the 70th birthday of author and poet Dr. Maya Angelou. We were two of 150 guests aboard the Seaborne Pride.

I will never forget that day. I was standing on the lower deck in the midst of a crowd having a personal moment. Earlier that morning I had breakfast with the renowned songwriting couple Nick Ashford and Valerie Simpson, or Nick and Val as I now was privileged to call them. Within the past three days I held conversations with the likes of the late Coretta Scott King, widow of the great civil rights leader Rev. Martin Luther King Jr.; Dr. Dorothy Height, civil rights icon and chairwoman of the National Council of Negro Women; Dr. Johnetta Cole, who was the president of Spelman College; Susan Taylor, then Editor-in-Chief of Essence magazine, and Gayle King,

Courage

Oprah's best friend and Executive Editor of "O", the magazine.

I marveled at the beauty of the water. In every direction, north, south, east and west, the water touched the sky. Never in my life had I been surrounded by so much water. I whispered to God, *"Thank you for allowing me to see and experience so much. Thank you for giving me such a full life."* I took a deep breath and looked around as the warmth of the sun's rays absorbed into my skin. I noticed the great music producer Quincy Jones standing on the upper deck and Ambassador Andrew Young and his wife taking a stroll on the lower deck. *"Thank you, Lord!"* I was humbled and honored to be a part of this event, to be one of the *"boat people,"* as Oprah and Maya had dubbed us.

This particular morning the ship had dropped anchor and water games were scheduled for the day. I was standing in line waiting my turn to ride the banana boat; a 12-foot raft made for eight riders that

Courage

were pulled through the water at high speeds by a motorboat.

I was talking with Stedman Graham and gospel singer BeBe Winans, when the banana boat pulled in to pick up eight new passengers. Stedman noticed his daughter Wendy standing at the end of the line and beckoned her to come ride with him. This pushed me back a space so I now had to give up my life vest and wait for the next ride. I had no problem what so ever getting bumped back in line. You see, it was through Stedman that my wife and I made the invitation list. Stedman and I were business associates whose relationship turned into an exceptional friendship. I attended his leadership-training program and my company conducted personality profiles on his staff. I'm also featured in his book, 'Build Your Own Life Brand.'

I watched as everyone mounted the banana boat smiling, laughing and eagerly anticipating the adventure. The motorboat headed out into the

89

Courage

ocean and gradually picked up speed. Suddenly there was a loud SPLASH and the banana boat tipped over! All eight passengers were in the water. Everyone on the deck was laughing at the sight of those people splashing around; it was hilarious.

The laughter faded as one of the ladies shouted, *"Look at Nyaho. He's drowning!"* And there was Nyaho, a concert pianist who couldn't swim, bobbing up and down like a fishing lure fearfully fighting the water. Every time he surfaced, the waves hit him in the face and he started fighting harder – accelerating the process. Fear was all over his face. Even from the distance, I could see the terror in his eyes. I didn't think he would drown. Hell, he had on a life vest. But the more he fought, the more he went under.

More people on deck were focusing on Nyaho and panicking. *"Nyaho's drowning! Nyaho's drowning! Somebody do something."* Unfortunately the driver

Courage

of the motorboat had eight people to rescue and as fate would have it, Nyaho was the farthest away.

"Nyaho's drowning! Nyaho's drowning! Somebody do something." I looked around, and saw nothing but panic and confusion. I remembered hearing or reading somewhere that it was possible for a person to drown from a single glass of water. Without a second thought I made one of the boldest decisions in my life and leaped off the ship into the ocean!

"Oooh Whee, the water was cold!" I began to appreciate Nyaho's fear immediately. The awesome force of the ocean is incredible. The sheer power of tons upon tons of water moving in unison (seemingly against you) is unfathomable. Every wave seemed to pull me under. I suddenly realized this is the OCEAN!!! Sharks live here! Thousands of people have drowned in these waters! Ships have sunk in these waters! What in the HELL am I doing here?

Courage

Just as Fear was about to paralyze my body as well as my thoughts, I looked at Nyaho and I could see relief in his eyes. I could hear the cheers of encouragement from the people on deck; their entreaties seemed to get louder with every stroke as if someone was turning up the volume. I decided that Fear would not be an option.

I reached Nyaho and helped push him out of the water and into the motorboat. Once we were safely on the ship, I received numerous pats on the back and congratulations. The best of all was Nyaho, who sincerely thanked me for, *"saving his life."*

On the way to my room, I stopped to glance back at the ocean now calm and serene. Not more than five minutes earlier it was the sight of a near disaster, I was amazed at its drastic change. The series of events played over in my mind and I thanked God and marveled at my role. Many people watch television, movies, or read books and through fictional characters fantasize how they would

Courage

respond in certain situations. That April afternoon aboard the Seaborne Pride, I discovered that I possessed the courage to jump off of a ship in the middle of the ocean to save someone. Leadership and Courage are interdependent; separation diminishes them. A leader without Courage is of little use to anyone.

I've often been asked, *"How did you and Stedman meet. How did you become friends?"* Actually, its an interesting story best suited for the chapter on Destiny. But now seems like as good a time as any to tell it.

In the summer of 2006 my wife was pregnant with our second child. I was traveling to New York with the President of The Gallup Organization, Jim Clifton. We had a meeting scheduled with Bill Bratton, the New York Police Chief, who earlier graced the cover of Time magazine. It was my first trip with Jim as a Vice President of the company.

93

Courage

After checking into the hotel we met for dinner and during the small talk, I mentioned that I'd called home and no one answered. I jokingly told Jim Robin was probably having the baby; which really wasn't unlikely because our first child arrived seven weeks early. Jim became serious and told me if I didn't reach her that evening to catch the first thing smoking in the morning. *"If anything happens and you aren't there she will never forget."* I called my wife's sister and discovered Robin was indeed in the hospital. I cancelled the meeting and caught an early bird flight the next morning. I arrived home around 9:00am, ran in the house to drop off my luggage and found Robin sitting on the sofa eating bonbons. To my chagrin we were two more unfortunate victims of the infamous Braxton Hicks Contractions.

It didn't take long for Robin to make it clear that she was enjoying her time alone, with the bonbons. I wasn't sure if she really wanted/needed company but upon her insistence, I decided to go to work.

Courage

This was a deliberate decision because my office was fifty miles away in Lincoln, NE and I normally car pooled to work. My ride was long gone.

I drove into the office and the first thing I did was check the voice mail. I had message from a colleague in Chicago and I immediately returned her call. She wanted me to pick up Stedman Graham from a hotel and bring him to the Gallup offices. Stedman had a meeting scheduled with our Chairman, Don Clifton. She said, *"Paul, I don't want him to think he is the only black person in the city."* With no time to spare bolted to the hotel. After pleasant conversation during the ride, I passed Stedman over to Don once we reached the office. As I turned to walk away, Don said, Paul, I want you in this meeting.

It was a synergetic meeting that lasted over an hour. It concluded with me getting a special project to find areas of opportunity for The Gallup

Courage

Organization and Stedman Graham & Associates to do business.

A few trips to Chicago, a couple of lunches and several rounds of golf later, Stedman and I had developed a pretty good friendship. I accomplished my assignment by orchestrating profitable business exchanges for both organizations.

Stedman is one of my true friends: I've been through his training program and he included my story in his book, *Build Your Life Brand.* I am a regular in his Annual Golf Tournament and we have plans to collaborate on a project to empower African American men and boys.

It appears that Stedman and I were destined to meet. Consider the circumstances; if my wife didn't have Braxton Hicks Contractions, I wouldn't have been in the city. If I wasn't able to secure a seat on the early bird flight, I wouldn't have been in the office in time to pick Stedman up. I could have stayed

Courage

home with my wife, or had a cup of coffee when I arrived in the office. If I had not immediately listened to voice messages or instantly returned the call I would have been too late to pick him up. If Don hadn't decided to invite me in that meeting; Nyaho may have drowned.

Three beautiful ladies -- My wife, Robin, Maya Angelou and Oprah Winfrey

The Seabourn Pride

Stedman Graham

Chapter Seven

Perseverance

How much can you handle?

Perseverance is the internal fortitude to deal with life's problems; it's having a never quit attitude; that something inside that never gives in no matter how great the obstacle. Perseverance is an absolute must for a Purpose Living Leader.

The view at the top looks so much better if you overcome adversity to get there. To know the full joy of victory and truly savor the triumphs of high achievement, you must have the ability to persist through the rough times. Think about it, if mountains were smooth, they would be impossible to climb.

99

Perseverance

There are many clichés that tout the value of perseverance:

"A winner never quits and a quitter never wins,"
"Behind every dark cloud there is a silver lining,"
"It's always darkest right before the dawn,"
"The race is not won by the swift or the battle the strong; the victory goes to the one who endures."

They all mean the same thing; in order to win you have to stay in the race... This same principal applies to life.

Look at the example of the caterpillar and the butterfly. The final step of the caterpillar's transformation into a butterfly requires leaving the cocoon. The struggle to squeeze through the cocoon almost takes the young butterfly's life, leaving it exhausted and vulnerable to predators. The cocoon is one of nature's mysteries. Its sole purpose is to insulate and protect the caterpillar. It's strong enough to withstand the harsh conditions of winter,

Perseverance

but weak enough for an insect to break through. The butterfly's fight for freedom is an essential key in its development. The butterfly's wings are strengthened as it wrestles to get free. Without the struggle its wings would not develop properly and the butterfly would never be able to fly.

We are perfected through hardships and misfortunes mold our character. We dig in when we face difficulties and we use our heads most when times get hard. Our lives are full of perseverance building experiences; these events can shape and mold our character if we choose to learn from them.

My earliest recollection of persevering through adversity happened when I was 7 years old. My grandmother had taken my brother and me to the zoo. This was my first trip to the zoo and I had my heart set on seeing a gorilla. I had seen King Kong on television and I couldn't wait to see the giant 60-foot gorilla.

101

Perseverance

My brother, who was three years older than me, would run off and leave me after every exhibit. I was the typical younger brother desperately running behind him trying to keep up. I finally caught up with him at the lion's cage where he was standing on a three-foot brick landing with about 20 other kids. Everyone was holding on to an iron fence pointing and taunting the lion as he paced back and forth behind the bars of his cage.

Zoo standards were much different in 1965; the lion's cage was only ten feet from where we were standing. I squeezed in next to my brother and just as I secured a firm grip on the fence the lion stopped pacing. Without warning he lifted his hind leg and started urinating on the kids who were standing on the landing. For some reason, God only knows why, he directed his stream with laser beam accuracy at my forehead. As the other kids jumped down to safety, I stood there petrified, holding on to the fence for dear life. The force of his blast would have knocked me off the landing onto my back. I

Perseverance

had no choice but to stand there and be a human fire hydrant. I must have looked like a water-skier being pulled through the water at high speed. (I'm glad they didn't have video cameras back then or I would have been a winner on "America's Funniest Videos.")

After what seemed like an eternity, the lion finally emptied his bladder. I stepped down from the landing soaked from head to toe, my face was stinging and the stench of lion urine was burning in my nostrils. Not only was I embarrassed; I was in pain. How many people on the planet can tell you what it feels like to be pissed on by a lion? Well, I can! The pressure of a 500-pound lion urinating in your face is anything but pleasant. It's like rotating the nozzle of a water hose so the spray will shoot the farthest; holding it about six inches from your forehead and turning the water pressure on full blast. Now, imagine doing this to a seven-year-old child.

Everyone was pointing at me and laughing. I looked for my brother. I needed support, someone to run to for security to share the pain and embarrassment. My eyes finally located him and he was laughing just as hard as everyone else. His response hurt and I couldn't understand why he was amused at my humiliation. My eyes immediately filled with tears.

The floodgates were about to open and the teardrops were ready to fall when someone yelled, "Its Little Black Sambo," and the crowd burst into hysterical laughter! For those of you who don't know or remember, Little Black Sambo was a controversial book that was banned from public school libraries. The story was about a young African boy who was being chased by a pack of lions. Little Black Sambo ran around and around a tree until he turned into butter... Did I mention that it was 1965 in Omaha, Nebraska? We were probably the only black family at the zoo that day. I bit my lip and decided no one would have the pleasure of seeing

Perseverance

me break down, no one... I was determined not to cry.

Thank God, my grandmother arrived. She immediately rushed over to help. She ushered me to a water fountain and started washing me off using paper napkins from her purse. Then she made me stand in the sun until I dried off. My clothes dried quickly, but they radiated the putrid smell of lion urine. Every breath invited the urge to vomit. I wanted to go.

Without speaking a word, we started walking down the path toward the exit. When people's faces showed disgust after taking a whiff of me, I held my head high. Even when my grandmother and brother distanced themselves so they wouldn't have to smell me, I didn't cry. I completed the longest and loneliest walk of my life at seven years of age. I kept my shoulders straight, my chin up and my face dry.

Perseverance

At the time I didn't know how much that experience would prepare me for the future. God allowed me to experience one of life's most embarrassing moments at an early age. I was able to stand tall and not wither while being used as lion kitty litter. I was able to maintain my composure while being ridiculed. I experienced the sting of rejection and the loneliness of isolation without shedding a tear. There's an old saying, *"That which doesn't kill you, will only make you stronger."* The memory of this experience helped sustain me later in life when I tossed my hat in the political arena.

Everyone handles their troubles differently; some kids turn to drugs or alcohol. Others rebel against their parents and society; many abuse their bodies with sex or cigarettes. And some kids even consider suicide. The key to overcoming any obstacle is perseverance.

Puberty is an awkward time in which teens mature into adults; it's rife with uncomfortable moments.

Perseverance

Character, the foundation for adulthood, is shaped during the teen years. Unfortunately, these experiences are not one time events; they last for extended periods of time, even years.

I was in the eighth grade when my parent's divorce was finalized. The separation was civil and both my brother and I were pleased with my mother's decision to leave my father. The tension in our home was very thick and there was an increase in the frequency of fights between my parents. I loved my father, but there was too much anxiety in our house and I hated to see my mother abused.

My mother, brother, and I grew apart as we explored our new freedom. My mother's focus shifted internally to her own needs and desires. She started going out more and coming home later. She cooked infrequently, and we spent less time together. My brother was a freshman in college; he was into his guitar, his band, experimenting with drugs and girls. He was the poster child for Sex,

107

Perseverance

Drugs and Rock & Roll. My escape was football. I was going to play in the NFL.

My parents had been divorced about a year when my mother started dating. My father, whose infidelity led to their break up, became obsessed with my mother once he knew she was seeing someone else. There is an old saying, *"You don't miss the water till the well runs dry."* Many an evening he would come by the house, wake me out of a sound sleep and take me by someone's house where my mother's car was parked. We would sit and watch the house. I hated seeing my father, a former pillar of strength bend to the power of love. He would call our house and my mother would talk to him, but I could tell by her conversation she had absolutely no plans for reconciliation.

My mother started seeing one guy pretty regularly his name was Eddie. He was pretty cool, a snappy dresser and a smooth talker. He treated my mother with respect and he won my favor. He taught me

Perseverance

how to drive and he seemed to like having me around. As their relationship grew, my father could see my mother was never coming back to him. He could probably tell that I liked Eddie also.

One evening, my father came by the house unannounced while Eddie was visiting. Supposedly, his reason for stopping by was to see me. I was awakened by the doorbell and heard my mother tell Eddie to go into the back bedroom. She answered the door, and I heard my father say, *"Where's Paul?"* As I was getting myself together, I heard a slight scuffle. I walked out of my room in time to see my father searching for the man he thought was taking his family. He walked past me to my mother's bedroom.

Eddie was bracing the door with his body from inside the room. When my father hit the door with his forearm, it flew open and I saw Eddie fall to the floor. I remember my father saying, *"Man, what are you doing in my house with my kids?"* I thought,

Perseverance

"Oh no, Eddie's going to get beat down!" My father was an ex-football player with a vicious temper. I wanted to stop him, but I was petrified. I could neither move nor speak. Eddie said, *"Don't make me do this. Please don't make me do this."* Again, my father said, *"Man, what are you doing in here with my kids?"* He took a step toward Eddie and suddenly there was a muffled *"POP!"*

The air in the house immediately filled with the heavy, smell of gunpowder. My father took about three steps backward and fell, right at my feet. Eddie pulled out his gun and shot my father in the shoulder, and the bullet lodged behind his neck. My mother called 911, my brother got a towel, and I stood there frozen, as did Eddie. All Eddie could say was, *"I didn't want to shoot you, man. Why did you make me shoot you?"*

The ambulance arrived and my father refused to let them carry him out. He demanded to walk on his own. My brother rode with him to the hospital and

Perseverance

the only words my father said were, *"I was some place I had no business being."*

We spent the rest of the evening at the police station. We were individually questioned in private rooms. Each of us had to take a lie detector test. It was a cold, sterile experience. No one seemed to care about our feelings.

The next few days were a whirlwind. Relatives on my father's side wanted to know what happened. Rumors circulated that my mother set my father up. There was tension between my mother and Eddie. Everyone at school wanted to know what happened. Once the word got out, I was dealing with questions like, *"Hey, Paul. I heard your mother shot your father. Is that true?"* My mother's boyfriend had just shot my father. Sorting out my feelings was very difficult.

I went to visit my father in the Intensive Care Unit of the hospital and I remember walking into his

Perseverance

room and being intimidated by all the machines and equipment. As I rounded the corner, I heard this loud wheezing noise like an old furnace. I saw my father sitting up in the bed with tubes coming out of his nose and bandages around his neck. Nurses were frantically running around grabbing oxygen and calling for help. As he was gasping, fighting to breathe, he looked up and saw me staring at him. In the middle of his struggle for air, he waved me out of the room. I later learned his wound had swollen and was putting pressure on his throat, shutting off his supply of air. One of the nurses escorted me out of the room and that was the last time I saw my father alive.

My father's death unraveled the last shreds of my dysfunctional family. The drama that surrounded his funeral was unforgettable. My father's family, hurt and upset about the loss, constantly asked questions and made comments about my mother; this made it uncomfortable to be around them.

Perseverance

There were too many of my relatives focusing on my father's insurance policies and rental properties.

My brother seemed ambivalent to the whole situation, and my mother was on the verge of a nervous breakdown. I felt like every grown person I had learned to depend on was self- absorbed with how my father's death affected him or her. At age 14 I lost my father and I had no one to lean on. Every time I opened up to someone, we ended up talking about his or her feelings.

My mother and I didn't spend much quality time with each other after my father's death and our relationship started to deteriorate. Her relationship with Eddie ended shortly after the funeral and she eventually started seeing someone else. I couldn't understand her need for male companionship. I felt she should have focused more attention on me. I guess I was a constant reminder to her of my father at a time when she was ready to leave the past behind and start over.

Perseverance

It was during this period of my life that I first experimented with drugs and alcohol, lost my virginity, considered running away from home and even contemplated suicide.

But behind every dark cloud there is a silver lining. In the midst of my mistakes a calming voice told me I could and should do better. Like a moral compass it constantly directed me towards righteousness. As I grew older, I learned this was the voice of the Holy Spirit ministering to my soul.

This was the period of my life when I developed a personal relationship with Jesus Christ. I joined a church, got baptized and moved forward leaning on the Lord.

This was the most difficult period of my life. I was able to rise above the circumstances by leaning and depending on God. He carried me through the valley of despair. In order to win, it's an absolute must to stay in the race...

114

Perseverance

"One night I had a dream. I dreamed I was walking along the beach with the LORD. Across the sky flashed scenes from my life. For each scene I noticed two sets of footprints in the sand. One belonging to me and the other to the LORD.

When the last scene of my life flashed before me, I looked back at the footprints in the sand. I noticed that many times along the path of my life there was only one set of footprints. I also noticed that it happened at the very lowest and saddest times of my life.

This really bothered me and I questioned the LORD about it. "LORD you said that once I decided to follow you, you'd walk with me all the way. But I have noticed that during the most troublesome times in my life there is only one set of footprints. I don't understand why when I needed you most you would leave me."

The LORD replied, "My precious, precious child, I Love you and I would never leave you! During your times of trial and suffering when you see only one set of footprints, it was then that I carried you."

Perseverance

FOOTPRINTS IN THE SAND
Author Unknown

It's life's duty to push you to the limit. The only way to know your true strength is to hold on as long as you can. A Leader who waivers during adversity will have minimal success; choosing the path of least resistance seldom results in a victory.

Chapter Eight

Faith

What keeps you moving forward?

Faith is an absolute must for a Purpose Living Leader. In the midst of a fire, when things are not going according to plan, when the situation looks bleak and support is waning; doubt and uncertainty will surface and the opposition will rear its ugly head. In these situations, it's Faith alone that enables a Purpose Living Leader to stay the course.

Faith empowers you to stand firm when everything around you says run; it's the foundation for trust, it's the feeling married people want to have towards their spouse. Next to a sharp pencil and an eraser, faith is the most important tool a student needs in the classroom when taking a test. The bible defines faith as the belief in things hoped for and the evidence of things unseen.

117

Faith

Leaders must have faith. The successful achievement of a worthwhile goal or aspiration will test all four elements of the Purpose Living Leadership equation. If a leader has a <u>Vision</u>; a mental picture of where they are going and what they are to accomplish. If there is an altruistic <u>Purpose</u> behind that vision, then the <u>Courage</u> to stand and <u>Persevere</u> becomes easier. But Faith is the ingredient that binds everything together.

Many of us place our faith in people, governments, businesses and money. If the truth were told, we have been let down more than we care to admit. Personally, I have found there is nothing more dependable than the Lord. The bible says he will never leave you or forsake you. Jesus Christ is a rock that never moves; no matter what the circumstances he has always been there for me.

My faith in God was put to the ultimate test in 1991 when I ran for a political office. My first foray into politics was an unsuccessful bid for City Council. I

Faith

was a 31-year-old novice who chose to run against a ten-year incumbent, the first African American to hold the position.

I officially announced my candidacy in January to take advantage of the events recognizing Dr. Martin Luther King's Birthday. Declaring early provided a huge benefit; as the only person in the race I raised $9,000 dollars and registered 58 volunteers within three weeks. The most money my opponent had raised in any of his past three victorious elections was $5,000.

My strategy was to blanket the community with literature. I wanted every discussion concerning the race for City Council to begin with my name. I was at the Metropolitan Community College MLK luncheon with three volunteers shaking hands and handing out brochures; the University of Nebraska's MLK panel discussion with five volunteers; the Creighton University MLK luncheon with eight volunteers; the Ministerial Alliance annual MLK

119

Faith

Dinner with ten volunteers, and the City of Omaha's MLK celebration with 15 volunteers! Campaigning was becoming so popular that my volunteers were fighting with each other to hand out materials.

The Mayor attended three of those events and witnessed for himself the excitement and the growing number of supporters. He approached me during the Cities celebration and asked, *"You are serious about this aren't you?"* I said, *"Absolutely, I plan to win."* This was the first and only conversation I had with the Mayor during my campaign.

A few days later the Mayor and my opponent were having a public dispute and the Mayor made this comment; *"The Councilman's position is political. He's only taking this stand because he is in the race of his life against newcomer, Paul Bryant."* The newspaper published the Mayor's comments and my campaign was immediately legitimized.

Faith

Excitement swept through my headquarters. We had been campaigning for only a month and according to the Mayor, the ten-year incumbent was in *'the race of his life.'*

The following week I had my first fundraiser, *"Businesses for Bryant."* My strategy was to lock down the business community to gain a superior financial advantage. Getting their support was picking the low hanging fruit. I was the Business Development Officer for a large bank in the community and my job was to build relationships with company owners.

The day before the event an article appeared in the paper listing the 15 companies who were the hosts for my fundraiser. Two days after the event I received a call from one of the hosts, the President of the Omaha Economic Development Corporation. He advised me to meet with, THE SENATOR.

Faith

The Senator was the political King Pin in the black community. He was in his 21st year serving as the only African American in the legislature for the State of Nebraska. He was an icon in the community. He graduated from the Creighton University Law School and rose to prominence during the unrest of the 60's. He single handedly dominated the legislature with his knowledge of parliamentary procedures and his mastery of the filibuster. He was the Jesse Jackson of Nebraska.

In 2007, after 38 years in the legislature, the state voted in term limitations specifically to get him out of office. His trademark was playing the race card, lifting weights and wearing tight sweatshirts. He worked out, he was buffed and he wore sweatshirts everywhere; on the floor of the legislature, on television and even to the White House. In his opinion suits were clothing of the master and those who wore them were sellouts.

Faith

I scheduled a meeting with the Senator at a location of his choice. He chose the Spencer Street barbershop. The barbershop was once a political hot spot in the hood; it's where the young Senator cut hair before he entered the legislature. It was also the location where he was interviewed in the award winning 1960's documentary 'A Time for Burning.'

The choice of this location was a power move. A stranger to the community would not be comfortable in the heart of the hood in the Spencer Street Barbershop, especially after dark. This was a strategic meeting place sure to intimidate an outsider. For me, it was home, my Grandparents lived around the corner.

I entered the barbershop in great spirits. I had close to 70 volunteers and had just raised $4,500 at the business fundraiser. My high-powered political engine was only idling; it had not yet been shifted into drive. I didn't know why the Senator wanted to

123

Faith

meet with me; I didn't need to kiss the proverbial political ring. I had already done that a year ago.

My wife and I invited the Senator to our home for dinner a year earlier when I made the decision to run for office. We had an excellent time; the Senator was an engaging dinner guest and was very encouraging when he heard of my interest in running for City Council. He said, *"Run, the Councilman hasn't done anything for the community in a long time."* He asked me if there was anything in my past that someone could use to discredit me, He said, *"Politics is a dirty game and you need to have a thick skin."* I shared with him that ten years earlier when I was in college I had sold drugs. (You can read all about it in my next book)

I told him I didn't have a habit and was never arrested, but it was something I had done. The Senator asked if I still used drugs and I replied, *"No,"* he asked if I still sold drugs, and I said,

Faith

"No;" He asked, *"How long ago did you quit?"* I told him, *"Ten Years ago."* He said, *"Then don't worry about it, that was ten years ago, it was only a youthful indiscretion."*

I knew the Senator would be impressed; there I was, a year later with money in the bank, yard signs, brochures and a host of volunteers. I was a man of my word, many people talk about what they want to do, but I was taking steps to make it happen.

The Senator's endorsement would have been a major political triumph. I walked into the barbershop that evening fully expecting the wise old sage, the God Father of North Omaha, to share his wisdom and offer me his support. I couldn't have been more wrong...

I entered the room with a Tiger Woods smile and my hand extended. The Senator met me at the door, he wasn't smiling and he didn't shake my hand. He stared me directly in the eye and started in on the

125

Faith

most aggressive verbal assault I have ever heard. His exact words: *"You think you have us fooled, but you don't. You better drop out of this race. If you don't, I will make you look like the biggest Traitor, Turn Coat, Flunky, Puppet, Pawn, House Nigga, Uncle Tom that this community has ever seen. Every black person in this community will lose respect for you. And once we do, those white people you work for won't be able to use you anymore and you will lose your job. You have a lot of patsies around you; they are going to tell you to stay in the race, but they aren't the ones who will be in the meat grinder. If you stay in this race, I WILL CRUCIFY YOU!"*

I will remember his opening statement for the rest of my life... I was in total shock! My attempts to gain an understanding only seemed to make things worse. I think he was upset because white people owned the majority of the businesses hosting my fundraiser. He accused me of being a patsy for the Mayor even though I had only spoken with the

Faith

Mayor one time in my life. To this day I have no idea what set him off.

We talked for close to an hour and it didn't get much better. *"If you stay in this race your drug past is going to come out! You will be finished in this city. When I'm through with you, you won't be able to find another job. I'll bet that pretty little wife of yours will leave you. You will have to leave town at night under a cloak of shame and disgrace. I've done it before and will have no problem doing it to you!"* "But, Senator, what have I done?" *"It doesn't matter, I will create a straw man and I'll keep attacking that straw man. The majority of the people don't read; they will believe whatever I tell them."* He concluded that I was a pawn of the white community and could not be trusted.

I sincerely felt God had blessed me with talents that would benefit my district. I was a bridge builder for a community that was isolated. I genuinely believed I had something of value to contribute. I

127

Faith

graduated from college with two masters' degrees, worked several years with a large local bank and served the community as a civic volunteer on several boards. I thought politics was a direction God wanted me to take.

I left the barbershop crushed and demoralized. If the Senator publicly opposed me there was no way I could win the election. I shared the events of the evening with my wife and she reassured me of her support regardless of my decision. The next day I called the Senator and scheduled another meeting at the barbershop. We spent a couple of hour's together riding around the community in his car. I told him I was leaning toward dropping out of the race and he assured me that my decision was the best thing for the community. He comforted me like a councilor and even volunteered to stand with me at a press conference to announce my resignation. *"I'll stand with you, I'll tell them that forces outside our community were trying to influence our decisions and we were smarter than*

128

Faith

that. You tell them that your resignation is the best thing for the community."

I met with an attorney friend, one of my campaign insiders and shared with him my dilemma. His professional advice for me was, *"It seems your only options are how you want to back out. I suggest you back out quietly."*

After another sleepless night I told my wife that I was going to withdraw from the race. I listed all the reasons I thought it was the best thing to do and she listened attentively. She said she would support whatever decision I decided to make, but there was a look in her eyes that I didn't like. It wasn't the kind of look any husband wants to see from his wife. It wasn't intentional, but it was unmistakable. I interpreted it as the look of shame. I felt like I had lost her respect.

I went to work in a cloud of confusion. I sat in my office unsure of what to do, so I prayed. I asked

Faith

God for direction; to give me a sign, show me what he wanted me to do. As soon as I finished my prayer I opened my desk and pulled out a pamphlet of bible verses someone had handed me on a street corner downtown months earlier.

I open the pamphlet and there were two verses. On the first page it said, *"Though your sins be as scarlet, I will make them as white as snow."* The verse on the second page said, *"Those of you that are heavily laden, come onto me and I will give you rest."* The hairs on the back of my neck stood up... It seemed like God had personally delivered a message to me! I immediately called the television stations and told them to send their news crews to my campaign headquarters. I was going to give them a story to lead their evening news with.

It was a major controversy in 1991 for a political candidate to be mixed up with drugs. This was before President Clinton admitted to smoking but not inhaling marijuana. With the cameras rolling, I

Faith

voluntarily confessed my past drug involvement. *"Someone in this community has been digging through the garbage and they found something. They have informed me that if I don't drop out of this race they are going to make this information public. Well, I am going to empty my own trash. Ten years ago I was involved in the vicious triangle of buying, using and selling drugs. I'm ashamed of it, I can't change it, all I can do is use my life as an example to young people that you can make mistakes and still do something positive with your life."*

That press conference changed my life; I was the lead story on the evening news for all three-television stations. The next morning my picture was on the front page of the newspaper with this headline: **Council Candidate Dealt Drugs.** I became an instant celebrity for all the wrong reasons. My candidacy became a polarizing topic within the community. Folk were either adamant supporters or vocal opponents. Whenever I went out

Faith

in public, heads would turn and people would glance over at me and point. It seemed that everyone knew my name and they all had an opinion.

The next four months of my life were more up and down than the Dow Jones. From that moment forward, reporters wanted interviews; talk shows wanted me as a guest and newspapers wanted to do follow-up stories. The problem with my newfound popularity was that everyone wanted to talk about my drug past. No one cared about my reasons for running for office. My education and economic development programs never found the light of day.

Life wouldn't have been so bad if dealing with "gotcha" questions from the media were the extent of my suffering. However, the Senator and his cronies had begun a community wide smear campaign. It seemed like the Senator was the keynote speaker at every event that summer and he used every podium to run me down. He composed

Faith

a letter detailing his opinions of why I was unqualified for the position and printed the slanderous document on official State letterhead. These half-truths were mailed to the president of my bank, my pastor and to other community leaders. His followers passed this propaganda out on bus stops and in restaurants. They even staged rallies urging the people not to let a 'drug dealer' represent the community.

The Senator went as far as to bracket a banking bill in the legislature, which gave him uninterrupted minutes to talk. He said the only reason he was voting against the bill was because the bank I worked for was supporting it. He then trashed me on the floor of the legislature to the rest of the governing body. After extending me an invitation to meet him in an alley, he withdrew his bracket. His ramblings were officially recorded in the daily record. Not only did I have to campaign against a ten-year incumbent but I also had a twenty-year

Faith

State Senator on the sidelines throwing bombs at me.

Looking back, I guess I was naive. I unknowingly issued a challenge to the established political machine. The Councilman received endorsements from both African American school board members as well as the person who later became the first African American County Commissioner. I did mention that this was my first foray into politics, didn't I?

This was definitely one of the most difficult periods in my life. The number of volunteers on my team dropped from seventy down to five! Some of them joined the other team to ensure their names would not find their way on the Senators hit list. The word on the street was that anyone on my team would suffer the wrath of the Senator.

I was amazed at the inexcusable silence from the alleged community leaders. A major feud was

Faith

happening on the community's front lawn and they didn't have anything to say about it. Prior to the election I had served on the boards of the Urban League, the Great Plains Black Museum and the North YMCA. I was well known and had done a considerable amount of community service. Certainly the opinion leaders would have my back, I'd served with them, they knew me... In private they gave verbal support, but in public they distanced themselves. I felt betrayed and cut off by the people I thought were allies.

The hypocrisy was that less than five years earlier I worked as the Assistant Project Coordinator on a Federal Grant in Washington DC; The National Drug Control Strategy Development Grant for Law Enforcement Executives. The grant was a cooperative effort between the Drug Enforcement Administration, the International Association of Chiefs of Police, and the Bureau of Justice Assistance to identify the drug problem in America. I didn't understand how I was able to pass the

135

Faith

vetting process for three national law enforcement agencies, and serve as the second in command on a federal grant, but was not qualified to serve in my community.

Five years after the campaign I started the International Division for Public Safety for the Gallup Organization and hired Lee Brown as a consultant to my division. Lee was the former police chief in New York, Atlanta and Houston and he previously served as the Drug Czar in President Clinton's administration. The irony of it all; the top drug enforcement officer in the country, a former member of the president's cabinet had no problem working with me, but certain members of my community could not. I understand how Martin Luther King felt when he said, *"In the end it's not the racist words of hatred from the staunch segregationist that we will remember, in the end what we will remember is the appalling silence of our good friends."* Thank God Barack Obama didn't decide to start his political career in Omaha,

Faith

Nebraska. He never would have made it past the Senator...

I had my fill of the treachery and backstabbing and was close to folding under the pressure and stress of the political grind. The Senator's smear campaign was starting to affect my friends and family. I had to physically calm a friend after one debate. Tammy was in tears as she boldly defended my honor against an off duty police officer. She lost her temper and was ready to throw down; this was the first time I realized how personal this campaign had become for my faithful supporters. At another debate, security was needed to escort one of my cousins from the room.

I was doing my best to appear confident, putting a positive spin on the negative public opinion attack while enduring the betrayal of false friends. But the truth is I was tired of taking the high road and letting other people fight my battles. My perseverance had worn thin; I was ready to jump in

137

Faith

the dirt with everyone else. The public didn't know that the Senator was once married to my cousin. Many of my older relatives had willingly shared unflattering stories of the Senators spousal and parenting skills. The kind of stories the media would love to run with... I knew this was an inappropriate route to travel, but every slight and every negative comment brought me closer to retaliating.

I had just about reached the end of my rope and was ready to reciprocate with the negative campaign when two community leaders stepped forward like guardian angels. One of them was John Foster, the CEO and founder of The Mad Dads, a national grass roots organization that encouraged men to reclaim their communities. Mad Dads was a recipient of the Essence Award and had tremendous credibility. John was around the same age as the Senator and called him out, *"To hold a young man's past over his head, to try and black mail a young man who is trying to do something positive in the*

Faith

community is criminal!" John's support allowed me to see that all the elders in the community had not written me off.

The other angel was Pastor William Barlow, of the Grace Apostolic Church. Grace Apostolic was a storefront ministry with a young growing congregation. Pastor Barlow was a fiery eloquent minister who was a master of words. *"The Black experience is about taking life's toughest body punches, getting knocked down and still getting up off the mat. Malcolm knew that, Martin knew that and Paul Bryant and his supporters know that!"* His blunt, tell-it-like-it-is style motivated me to stay strong and keep fighting.

I will never forget John Foster or Pastor Barlow. These men were crutches; they came to my aid and held me in position when I was not able to stand by myself. God places people in our lives for many different reasons; some are with us always and others are with us just for a season. These men

Faith

helped me stay focused on the high road. They showed me you can't get in a ditch with someone without getting dirty yourself. To this day my mother tells me her proudest moment was watching me stand tall on the high road to withstand the Senator's attack.

When the smoke from the campaign-from-hell finally cleared, I lost the election. I finished second out of four candidates in the primary but lost in the general election. Nevertheless, I lost with dignity and held my head high. I was a novice. This was my first election and I took on an incumbent City Councilman and a State Senator. Every black elected official in the state of Nebraska was on the other team and I still earned 40% of the votes.

President Theodore Roosevelt's quote titled, Man in the Arena, given by, in Paris, France on April 23, 1910 summarizes my feeling about that campaign.

Faith

"It is not the critic who counts; not the man who points out how the strong man stumbles, or where the doer of deeds could have done them better. The credit belongs to the man who is actually in the arena, whose face is marred by dust and sweat and blood; who strives valiantly; who errs, who comes short again and again, because there is no effort without error and shortcoming; but who does actually strive to do the deeds; who knows great enthusiasms, the great devotions; who spends himself in a worthy cause; who at best knows in the end the triumph of high achievement, and who at the worst, if he fails, at least fails while daring greatly, so that his place shall never be with those cold and timid souls who neither know victory nor defeat."

But this chapter isn't about politics, it's about Faith, *"the belief in things hoped for and the evidence of things unseen."* You see, I knew I would lose the election when I walked out of the Spencer Street Barbershop. Faith in God was the only reason I was

141

Faith

able to carry on. I kept reading those two passages in that pamphlet; *"Though your sins be as scarlet, I will make them as white as snow. Those of you that are heavily laden, come onto me and I will give you rest."* I had faith that at the end of the day I would come out all right.

My battle was bigger than the election. I felt a need to stand up against the Senator and face the fire even though I knew I was going to get burned. This may sound crazy, but as I stood there and listened to the Senator profess everything he planned to do, it felt like I was having a close encounter with Satan. There was something wicked, something evil about his presence. The hair on the back of my neck stood up. I felt danger like standing on the ledge of a tall building. And yes, I'll admit it I was intimidated.

I read Psalms 27 every morning to prepare myself for the challenges of each day.

Faith

Psalms 27, verse 1-3: *The Lord is my light and my salvation – whom shall I fear? The Lord is the stronghold of my life – of whom shall I be afraid? When evil men advance against me to devour my flesh, when my enemies and my foes attack me, they will stumble and fall. Though an army besieges me, my heart will not fear; though war break out against me, even then will I be confident.*

After the election my personal stock went through the ceiling. The bank promoted me to an Officer. The word on the street was that I would be fired after the election. Then I was named one of the Ten Outstanding Young Omahans. Not long after that award, the Mayor appointed me to the City Personnel Board and shortly after that I received a full scholarship to the Creighton University Law School.

Numerous people told me they admired my courage for standing up to the Senator and my honesty for admitting my past. All I know is, I put my Faith in

Faith

the Lord and immediately after the campaign I was being showered with blessings. The most incredible blessing however, came months after the campaign; the day my wife told me we were expecting our first child.

Nothing in life is closer to a miracle than having a baby. The joyful news of our first child required none of the Faith needed when my wife told me we were expecting number three...

The year was 2000, the beginning of the new millennium. The Y2K scare was unfounded. Armageddon didn't come and neither did any of the other chaos and havoc that was predicted for the turn of the century. My household was healthy. The bills were paid and my wounds from the campaign were well healed. I wasn't mad at *n-o-o-body!* Little did I know a bomb was about to drop?

After finishing my routine of reading a bedtime story to my children, I kicked back in my easy chair

Faith

to watch television. Mid-way through my favorite program, my wife stood directly in front of the TV. Before I could protest, she looked me straight in the eye and informed me we were three months pregnant!

Within seconds, my thoughts started running the spectrum from jubilation to fear. On one hand I thought, *"Oh yeah, I'm the man! I'm 42 years old and I'm still making babies. I'm a ba-a-ad MAN! My genes are strong; my plumbing is good!"* And on the other hand I thought, *"Oh no, I'm 42 years old! Where in the world will I find the energy to raise another child? I will be 61 when this child graduates from high school. If she goes to Graduate School, someone will have to wheel me down the aisle for the ceremony! I thought we were finished with Pampers and car seats."*

Surprised, shocked, stunned, shaken; none of these words are strong enough to describe what I felt. I was however, astute enough to know that my

Faith

response in the next five seconds would have a direct and consequential effect on the peace and tranquility of my home. The last thing I wanted to do was mess this up.

My wife stood there observing my facial expressions and body movements. I knew she was going to judge every utterance. The tone, inflection and selection of my words would be dissected. All her senses were on alert, primed to pick up any negative vibe. I could tell that no matter how I responded, her instincts would be the final judge. The potential was high for a major mis-understanding.

I wrestled with my thoughts, *a 1% chance of getting pregnant on the pill. Why did we have to validate that statistic!* Then I looked into the eyes of the woman I loved and her ebony pupils pierced my soul. An internal voice said, *"Get up and embrace her."* Faithfully without hesitation, I jumped out of my chair, engulfed her with a hug and said, *"Thank*

Faith

God, what a blessing!" As I held her, I could feel the anxiety ease out of her body as she squeezed me tightly and said, *"Amen."*

Faith is one of the most valuable arrows you can have in your quiver. My faith is currently being pushed to the limit. As I write this paragraph I am torn between either accepting a lucrative job offer or declining to continue my work with the Wesley House Leadership Academy.

The financial crisis in America makes this opportunity extremely attractive. Investment banks are failing, commercial banks are merging and congress has authorized a multi-billion dollar financial bailout to help stabilize the volatile stock market fueled by the number of foreclosures resulting from sub-prime mortgages. Thousands of American workers have been laid off, retail sales are down, gas prices are up and unemployment rates are at a 14-year high. In short, the economy sucks! This is not a great time to be running a non-profit

Faith

business that relies exclusively on donations for survival.

I have served as the Executive Director for the Wesley House Leadership Academy for close to 4 years and have risen close to 1½ million dollars, but my efforts to bring the United Way back to the table have been unsuccessful. In 2003 the United Way contributed close to $300K to fund the Wesley House. Today they contribute nothing…

The vision for the future is clouded with skepticism. Without the United Way, we rely totally on the generosity of philanthropists and corporate contributions. It doesn't take an economist to predict donations will be more difficult to secure in 2009. We currently operate on a shoestring budget; it's only by the grace of God that we have been able to survive. I've had many sleepless nights without the pending financial crisis.

Faith

A Fortune 500 company offered me a position that will about double my salary! I'm torn between going for the money, the job security and career mobility vs. continuing my mission to nurture and develop future leaders. The prospect of leaving the students and reneging on the promise I made their parents weighs heavy on my mind.

The decisions I make not only affect the children and families at the Wesley House, they affect my wife and three children as well. Accepting the position at the Wesley House was a financial step backwards and my family is starting to feel the effects of my sacrifice. My youngest child has never been on vacation and I can't remember the last time I took my wife out to dinner. All of my investments are going south and my retirement account is down 30 percent. I'm not stupid; I realize financial problems are the number one cause for divorces. Every rational thought tells me this is the time to position myself for the future. I should take the job, rebuild my nest egg and wait for the economy to rebound.

These are scary and uncertain times and no one knows what tomorrow will bring. But I believe in my heart that I should decline the job offer... The rebirth of the Wesley House is a task God gave to me and my work is not complete. Even though the future looks bleak, I have faith that God will see me through. If it's God's will for the Wesley House Leadership Academy to close in 2009, then I'm obligated to go down with the ship.

Today is Tuesday, November 11th, 2008, and I officially turned down their offer. Time will tell if this was the correct decision. Throughout life when I have been confronted with situations and was unsure what to say or do, I've leaned on the Lord and he has always brought me through. I will put my faith in Jesus; if it is his will, the Wesley House Leadership Academy will prosper in the midst of America's financial crisis.

Faith

Dedication, conviction and devotion are the seeds of faith. Everyone has something they believe in. What is it for you? At the end of the day, when you're all alone, what is it that drives you? Why do you put forth the effort? Once your find your core beliefs you will find your faith.

> *"Faith, the belief in things hoped for and the evidence of things unseen. If God be for you, who can be against you? There is no wisdom, or understanding, or knowledge against the Lord."*
>
> *The Bible*

Court Rules
William Hurt
Wasn't Married

People Page 5

Exhibitor Says
Art Show Honors
Black History

Living Page 57

FRIDAY
FEBRUARY 22, 1991   EDITIONS
OUR 126TH YEAR
NO. 128   98 PAGES
25¢

Omaha World-Herald

Sunrise Edition

Bryant's Admission Stirs Controversy

Council Candidate Dealt Drugs

By Mike Reilly
World-Herald Staff Writer

Bryant... "I'm not proud of it."

Please turn to Page 12, Col. 1

U.S. Reports
New Successes
On Iraqi Armor

The Washington Post

GULF **WAR**

Gordon Walls, one of my
faithful supportes

Chapter Nine

Hope

Where will it lead, what will it bring you through?

Why are some people considered destined for success and others believed to be born losers? Are the circumstances in our lives predetermined? Are past experiences indications of our destiny? I don't know the answers to these questions; what I do know, however, is the ability to triumph over adversity is a universal characteristic that distinguishes winners from losers.

The age-old struggle between success and failure is a war fought on a battle field within the subconscious realm of the mind. Inadequacy and Inferiority are weapons of choice effectively used by failure. They produce a demoralizing state of mind that can surface anywhere, at any time.

153

Hope

Amongst anybody, they have the power to contain, detain and restrain talent. If allowed to grow in a fertile mind, they will evolve into insecurity. Insecurity will hold back and back down any attempt to succeed. The end result is a self- induced feeling of insufficiency; an inner numbness that says, *"you just don't measure up"*.

Hope is the most effective weapon in the battle against negativity. The Gallup Organization has research that identify hope as a predictor of grade point average, school attendance and high school credits earned. Optimistic, constructive, affirmative thinking will obliterate negative self-perceptions. Many people don't realize positive thinking has the power to shape morale. The dictionary describes hope as *"a feeling of confidence; expectation; to look forward to something believing that it will happen,"*...As a man thinks, so he shall be. If Faith is the confidence in things hoped for; then Future Focused Faith is Hope.

154

Hope

My past experiences lead me to the conclusion that our personalities become wired for success or failure during middle and high school. These are the years in which life deals us the cards of puberty, peer pressure and promiscuity; trump cards that have derailed many successful futures. Those who successfully navigate the teen-maze often share a common trait. They have a steadfast hope for a brighter future. Hope gives them security, a sense of well-being during uncertain times which allows them to explore their talents and fully engage in life.

I was able to overcome life's obstacles because of my Faith in God and an unwavering Hope in the future. When I was fourteen years old, I witnessed the fatal shooting of my father. At fifteen, I was falsely accused of rape, and at sixteen, I seriously considered suicide. I used and sold drugs regularly before I reached the age of twenty. I never talked with anyone in my family about higher education. For some reason, discussions about my future plans didn't happen. I don't know if it was lack of

155

concern or low expectations, but no one was interested in discussing my future.

On the flip side, The crowning achievement of my senior year was receiving a four-year football scholarship to (USC), after graduating from college, I was inducted into the Benson High School Hall of Fame, was presented the Alumnus achievement award from the University of Nebraska-Omaha, was selected to receive the College Marketing Award; was chosen as one of the ten Outstanding Young Omahan's by the Junior Chamber of Commerce and honored with the Martin Luther King "Living the Dream" Award from the Mayor of Omaha. From the streets to the suites, I've been there…

HIGH SCHOOL

When I was a kid I began to view my future through the lens of success after receiving the MVP Award

Hope

in midget league football. I envisioned myself having an exciting, professional football career fully equipped with fame and fortune. I received preferential treatment as an aspiring athlete. I can't deny it, teachers, administrators and parents liked me. I was popular with the student body; my self-esteem was extremely high.

However, when my father died, my vision for the future became less optimistic. I received $1,075 from my Dad's insurance policy and like a typical teenager; the money burned a hole in my pocket. I purchased a car two months after receiving the check. I was 15 years old, didn't have a driver's license and didn't know how to drive.

The very first day I went looking, I ran into Steve Stiles, the epitome of a used car salesman – pushy, fast-talking and unethical. Before I could blink, he had me signing the papers on a gray 1967 Pontiac Firebird convertible soon to be known as THE BIRD. Steve's memorable quote, *"look at that back seat, can't you see all the tail you're going to get back there."*

In its former life as a stock car, THE BIRD was geared up to burn rubber at the slightest touch of the gas pedal. The neighbors must have hated me because I burned rubber at every stop sign. At age 15, screeching tires was the coolest thing you could do with a car.

THE BIRD expanded my world; I was now in possession of an adult toy. My life changed the day I drove THE BIRD to Monroe Junior High School. While my classmates were walking home, I was giving rides. I was able to drive to other schools and make friends in other parts of the city. My classmates thought I had the coolest situation in the world. It must have looked great from the outside. I was 15 years old, owned my own car and had total freedom with no supervision. Yeah, there was plenty of swagger on the outside, but internally, I

Hope

was lonely, I missed my father and I longed for a traditional family.

The Bird offered unlimited mobility and it also introduced me to a different cast of characters. I became exposed to a much worldlier lifestyle. This extended network was just what I needed escape from the pain of my father's death; none of my new friends knew the story of my Dad getting shot by my mothers boyfriend... I started using marijuana on a frequent basis and my behavior became decadent, immoral and self-indulgent.

That fall when I started High School, my mind was in a totally different place. (This is your brain; this is your brain on drugs) A lot of kids had cars in high school so THE BIRD was not a novelty anymore. No longer "The Big Man on Campus," I had to establish myself all over again and I did a great job maintaining. Everywhere except on the football field. The area that provided my source of hope was now diminishing. The motivation to

159

Hope

sacrifice my body for the good of the team was no longer there. It was replaced with self-pity, heartache and loneliness.

My new source of identity became my relationships with girls. I had a girlfriend, her name was Janelle – hot and physical best describes our relationship. Every time we had the opportunity, we took it! We made Steve Stiles a prophet. The focus I used to give football was now diverted to her…

One day after school Janelle and I decided go to my house after school. The plan was for her sister to pick her up on her way home from cheerleading practice. When her sister arrived, my brother let her in the house; led her to my bedroom and told her to go in. She opened the door and caught Janelle and I studying *anatomy*. Totally embarrassed, she shut the door, walked out of the house and left. We were embarrassed, but didn't abort the mission.

Hope

Twenty minutes later, we heard the squealing of tires as her sister's car wheeled around the corner. She pulled in the driveway, jumped out of the car and said to Janelle, *"You're in trouble... Daddy's home!"*

Her father demanded his daughters to always come home together and this particular evening he came home early. At the time, he seemed excessively strict. Now that I have two daughters of my own, I understand his rationale completely. When he inquired about Janelle's whereabouts and was told where she was, he sent Janelle's sister to bring her home.

I gave Janelle a hug and told her everything would be alright. My reassurances carried little weight; I hadn't even met her father. I kissed her on the cheek and noticed the worried look in her eyes. In my wildest dreams I couldn't predict the drama the next day would bring.

Hope

During second hour there was a knock on the door. The teacher opened it and in stepped my mother. My teacher stepped out of the room and my mind started racing. *"Why was my Mother at school?"* I didn't have a clue what was going on, but I knew it couldn't be good. The last time I received a surprise visit from a relative was when my brother came to school to inform me our father had died. The teacher returned to the room and told me to take my books and leave with my mother.

Mom just started walking, she didn't say a word. I followed, taking my cue from her. We didn't talk. We just walked. When we reached her car, I noticed a police cruiser parked in front of the school. Two officers were standing in front of the building looking in our direction.

My mind was racing. *"Why was she here? Where was she taking me?"* I wasn't going to say a word until she spoke first. We had driven a short distance

Hope

when she asked, *"Do you know a girl named Janelle?"*

I said, *"Yeah, that's my girlfriend."* I remember thinking to myself, *"Man, things are really bad between us. You don't even know who I'm dating. Janelle has been over our house numerous times and you don't even know her."*

Then in a casual, unemotional tone, she asked this question. It seemed more like she was making a statement than asking. *"Did you rape her?"*

"RAPE, what? Rape? Rape? No, no, uh, uh, no... I didn't rape her!"

"Well, Janelle said you did. We are on our way to the police station."

I was paralyzed! I didn't know what to think or say. We drove to the police station in silence. I couldn't look at her and she didn't look at me.

163

Hope

When we arrived at the police station they were expecting us. I was escorted by an officer into a private room to be questioned. This was the very same room they questioned me in after my father was shot. A whirlwind of thoughts swirled through my mind. *"Why would Janelle lie on me? I thought we liked each other?"*

The officer interviewed me for about an hour, asking me very personal questions about Janelle and the events of the day before. I couldn't concentrate. This was the most serious trouble I had ever been in. I was in a daze. *"How could she accuse me of rape, we had been together many, many times..."* This had to be a mistake, but here I was answering questions at the police station. *"Did something happen to her? Should I try to protect her? Was she OK? Were they going to put me behind bars? "*

After exhausting me of every ounce of truth, the officer actually told me she believed my story. She cautioned me not to say one word to Janelle and she

Hope

said they would be in touch to inform us what would happen next.

Another silent ride and I was back at school. My mother and I never talked about it again; to this day, we have not discussed that incident.

I didn't know how to respond at school. The police told me not to speak to Janelle, so I didn't. When I saw her, she looked away. But her friends glared at me. It didn't take long for the story to hit the grapevine. Before the day ended, the buzz was, *"Paul Bryant raped Janelle!"*

Nobody in their right mind wants to be associated with a rapist. I became an instant outcast. I didn't have a stellar start the football team and the rape accusation officially flushed my reputation down the toilet with the football season. People glared at me and whispered. Many of the teachers and coaches treated me like pond scum.

Hope

Mentally I was in another place. The rest of that year, I looked at Janelle from a distance. I wanted so much to ask her what happened, but I heeded the officer's advice and didn't say a word to her. We never talked. It wasn't until years later that I discovered her family dropped the charges two days after I was questioned. Janelle broke down under questioning and told them she accused me of rape to avoid getting in trouble. I endured an entire year of school expecting the police to call summoning me to court.

Football, which had been the foundation of my hope didn't matter anymore. My lack of effort manifests itself into sub-par performance. I went through the motions at practice, but my head wasn't in the game. For the first time in years, I sat the bench. I was relegated to fourth-quarter action. The cleanup time after the game had already been decided. I was a scrub; a non essential member of the team. The coaches constantly rode my back. But the more they yelled at me, the more I retreated into a shell. I

Hope

didn't know if they felt I wasn't playing up to my potential or were they trying to run the rapist off the team.

Without anyone to communicate with, no one to talk me through the shame of having my name tarnished, or the pain of my father's death, I just shrugged my shoulders and held a pity party. In the back of my mind I wondered, *"If I would have worked out during the summer; If I hadn't smoked so much weed, If I had focused on my sport and not on Janelle, would it have made a difference?"*

The year ended. Summer started, and I was still depressed. I sulked around wearing my father's old clothes and staying to myself. I worked a nothing job as a dishwasher in a steakhouse restaurant and discovered what it means to be the low man on the totem pole. This job gave me firsthand experience with the class system. Dishwashers get no respect. We were low in seniority and treated as such. Cooks, waiters, hostesses and even busboys took

167

Hope

turns playing the obnoxious game of demeaning the dishwashers.

I totally lost my focus and direction. Not only did I loose respect and status that year, I lost my dream of playing in the National Football League. For years, Football had been my exit strategy. My aspiration was to play in the NFL, fully accompanied with fame and fortune. Now I didn't have any goals and hope was gone; washing dishes was the best I could do. I was spiraling downward and not a single person in my family had a clue.

My outlook on life became extremely negative. I accepted the reality of being alone and continued my pity party well into the summer. Morbid thoughts frequently ran through my head. At times suicide seemed like a viable option. I was a time bomb waiting to explode and not a soul in this world knew my mental state. Tragedies like the one at Columbine High in Colorado, where students arm themselves and start shooting at random, leave

Hope

everyone asking questions like: *"How did this happen? Why didn't their parents know?"* Many people don't realize how close they come to having a catastrophe in their own back yard.

My only entertainment outlet was the summer league basketball games until Janelle and her new boyfriend became regulars. Watching them walk in together holding hands tormented me. I hadn't spoken a word to her concerning the accusation and I needed closure. How dare she move on with her life? Seeing her look so happy was more than I could take. I was seething! I became obsessed with her. All I could think about was the fun we used to have and how it ended so abruptly. The last time we talked was at my house when I told her everything was going to be alright. How dare she move on?

I blamed her for the cloud of gloom and doom that was over my head. My life wasn't bad until she accused me of rape. Now I was a scrub on the football team, with a tarnished reputation, who

Hope

washed dishes for a living… I decided to crash her party. Why should she be happy while I was depressed? This dishwasher had reached his limit.

I developed a plan to make Janelle tell me why she lied on me and to scare the crap out of her new boyfriend. I intended to take my mother's pistol to a basketball game; lure them outside, and then point the gun at them. I was prepared to beat her boyfriend down if he didn't go along with the program, I would have loved to inflict a little pain with my hands. I had no intention of shooting anyone so I took the clip out of the gun. How was I to know a bullet remained in the chamber after the clip was removed?

I stood in my mother's bedroom getting psyched for the assignment at hand. Pointing the gun at myself in her full length mirror, *"You talking to me? Are you talking to me?"*

Hope

I took my mother's gun and planned to get some satisfaction. For some reason, on my way out of the room I spun around, pointed the gun at the bed and pulled the trigger. KA-POW! OH-MAN!!! Was I was shocked when the gun went off! I didn't know a bullet remained in the chamber after the clip was taken out. My heart was pounding so hard I thought it would explode. The room was thick with the smell of gunpowder. It was the same pungent smell coming from the same room where my father was shot. There was a huge black stain on my mother's comforter.

My mind started racing 500 miles an hour. *"Open the door. Get the smell out. Get a fan. Hurry up! Clean the comforter. What if you had pointed that at Janelle and pulled the trigger?"*

Then my thoughts took a morose twist. *"This is the same room your father was shot in. So what, if you pointed it at Janelle and pulled the trigger, she deserves it! Why don't you point the gun at yourself? Shoot yourself. Yeah, why don't you shoot yourself?"* I looked at my image in the mirror while that voice continued to prod. *"Shoot yourself. That will show them. Shoot yourself. They will be sorry they ever mistreated you. Shoot! Your family, those teachers, coaches and Janelle, they will all be sorry, SHOOT!"*

It pains me to write, that suicide seemed to make sense. If I died everyone would know how I felt, then they would regret how they ignored and mistreated me. That voice in my head kept talking, *"It won't hurt. It will happen so fast, you won't even feel it. Go ahead, don't be scared, SHOOT!"*

"Who will miss you? Does the team really need another benchwarmer? Your employer can find a dishwasher anywhere, it didn't take Janelle long to find another boyfriend. Nobody will miss you, SHOOT!"

Hope

I looked at the gun and decided to put in the clip, then another voice began to speak. It was a more calming, less demanding voice. It seemed to override the frenzy in my head. This voice had power and authority. It said, *"This is NOT what I have planned for you."* I looked at my image in the mirror and saw how pitiful it looked. My hand tightened around the gun. The voice spoke again, *"Listen to me. I will bring you through this valley."* I looked down at the gun in my hand, and then looked up at my reflection in the mirror. The voice said, *"LISTEN TO ME! You have a future ahead of you..."* The thought of suicide slowly dissipated...

Physically tired, I dropped to my knees, wept and prayed. Eventually, I got up, put the gun away, and cleaned my mother's comforter. I spent the rest of the evening alone, but not lonely. The voice of Hope continued to speak. It said, *"You are somebody and there is a purpose for your life."* From that moment forward, I began to listen to that voice. It still speaks to me, during quiet moments,

Hope

when I am alone it still talks to me. I believe it is the voice of God...

I hibernated the rest of the summer determined to regain my edge. When football practice started I was on a mission. Football once again became my ticket and it was time to cash in. I sent a loud message the first day of contact. *"So, you think I'm a rapist?"* WHAM! *"You think I have problems?"* KA-BLAM! *"You think you're better than me?"* CRUNCH! *"Bring it on!"* I delivered blows and accepted all challenges. I rediscovered my hope for a better future.

The coaches noticed the change, and so did my teammates. I was in the zone. It seemed like every play was in slow motion. My leadership skills started to surface again. I called the plays on defense and was one of the team captains. I loved the way the guys looked up to me in the huddle. They had total trust and confidence in me. There's nothing like success to help you find your place in

Hope

life. After spending my junior year as a third-class citizen, I had forgotten what it felt like to be on top.

Everyone thought I worked extremely hard over the summer and rededicated myself to the game. The truth -- I was just following the voice inside my head.

We started the season with three shutouts; we dominated other teams. I was on a roll, running the No. 1 defense in the city. My success on the field even carried over into school. Several teachers who couldn't look me in the eye a year earlier started talking to me again.

As the season progressed, so did my confidence. People treated me differently. I now recognized the value of a good name and how precious a reputation could be. I was better prepared to handle success after my experiences a year earlier. The swagger was back, but it was grounded in humility.

Hope

There's a thin line between confidence and conceit. I wanted there to be no doubt about which side of the line I straddled. I was earning respect again but knew every smiling face wasn't friendly. The higher up you go only means the air gets thinner and you have a farther distance to fall.

My team only lost one game that year, we were division champions. At the end of the season, I was selected to the All Metropolitan Football Team! This honor validated me as one of the best football players in the city and was shortly followed by a four-year full ride scholarship.

When I told my mother the good news we were both happier about me having an exit plan than a scholarship. My mother repeatedly told me I would have to depart from her house when I graduated from high school and I knew she meant it. It was a blessing to be able to leave without being put out. We were both relieved to know our parting would consist of hugs and kisses. She gave me one of

Hope

those deep embraces that mean so much more than words can say. I hugged her back and for the first time in years, we talked.

On my way out of her room, I paused and looked at my reflection in her full length mirror. Ten months earlier I was standing in the exact same spot with a gun in my hand contemplating suicide. Now I was standing tall, one of the best football players in the city with a four-year all expense paid football scholarship. I smiled at my reflection, took a deep breath, and said, *"Thank you, Lord."* I just realized he had carried me through a valley, I had plenty of hope for the future.

I'm embarrassed to admit I considered suicide. It scares me to think of how close I came to putting the clip back in that gun and pulling the trigger. No matter how strange it sounds, I know that voice was the voice of God. On a morbid summer night in 1975 that voice stopped me in my tracks and gave

Hope

me hope. It caused me to look at myself and make a change.

Chapter Ten

Influence

Are you using it properly?

Purpose Living Leaders must have influence. John Maxwell says, *"Influence is the single most important trait of any leader. A leader must inspire, motivate or encourage others to act, if he does not possess the ability to influence people he will not be leading long."*

A leader's ability to inspire people to act will directly impact their legacy. There are numerous examples both positive and negative. If Martin Luther King marched in the streets of the south by himself the Civil Rights movement would have failed; India would still be under British rule if Mahatma Gandhi protested alone and Nelson Mandela would still be in prison if he did not have legions of followers. Influence is a great

179

characteristic to possess. Unfortunately there are many examples of people who have abused it. Adolph Hitler, Reverend Jim Jones and Charles Manson each used their influence to persuade their followers to commit horrendous acts of murder.

In my opinion, Jesus Christ is the epitome of a Purpose Living Leader. His teachings were so imbedded in the minds of his followers that even when faced with prison, torture or death they felt obligated to share his wisdom. So strong was Jesus' influence that over two thousand years after his death, his knowledge is still being taught around the world...

Influence cannot be acquired through books or training, it's like courage either you have it or you don't. Influence can be observed through our daily interactions with others and can be detected early in our lives.

Influence

My earliest recollections of having the ability to influence others go back to Monroe Junior High School. This was a pivotal time in my life; the lens through which I viewed reality changed rapidly. It was a time of maturity. My voice changed, I started wearing an Afro and I discovered girls. Ahhhh, yes, Junior High School is when I first developed a swagger.

The ninth grade football team was my opportunity to see if I could perform on a bigger stage. Winning the Ricky Smith Trophy in the eighth grade and having my picture in the paper with Gale Sayers bestowed me with a reputation as one of the best football players in the city. This was an opportunity to showcase my talent on another level. I rose to the occasion, was elected team captain and started on both offense and defense. However, personal achievements didn't mean very much because our team was mediocre. Our record was 3 wins and 3 losses for the season, but we should have won 5 games.

Influence

Our problem was the lack of leadership. We had an unproven coach who recently graduated from a small college. This was his first job. He had no prior coaching experience and no familiarity with black kids who comprised 40% of his team. For many of the players, both black and white, this was our first time playing on an integrated team. Thus we had all the ingredients necessary to create one combustible situation.

There is a great movie titled "Remember the Titans." Denzel Washington plays the role of Coach Boone in a true story about a high school football coach in Virginia. Coach Boone successfully leads his team through the challenges of integration. After overcoming numerous obstacles, his team unifies. They start to recognize their similarities instead of their differences and the team goes on to win the state championship during his first year as coach. Well, the story of the 1973 Monroe Mustangs is a case study on how to fail.

Influence

Our coach played favorites with the white players, which caused a major problem for the black players. A black player would run the ball close to the goal line and then the coach would replace him with a white player to score the touchdown. Whenever we had 10 yards or less for a score he would make a total rotation of the running backs. Most of the black players didn't start and in three games none of us had scored a touchdown. But we were the ones on the field at the end of the game desperately trying to save the ship when our team was behind. These tactics were frequent and predictable. His coaching decisions evolved into problems... The black players didn't have issues with the white players. We had a problem with losing games while our most talented players were sitting the bench.

Can you imagine the Chicago Bulls in their heyday not playing Michael Jordan? What would the PGA be like today if Tiger Woods were no longer allowed to play Golf? This may sound impractical today, but there was a time when discrimination

Influence

was that blatant. I personally experienced this type of racism. Black kids weren't allowed to start at the quarterback position no matter how talented they were.

We mumbled, grumbled and complained, but the response from our coach was that we needed to be team players. As the captain I was privy to the feelings of my teammates and I knew their level of frustration was high. A midseason loss ticked me off and I couldn't contain my disappointment any longer.

I decided to protest by loafing through practice. If the coach didn't want to win then why should I go 100%? I felt there was no need to go all out. The coach started riding my back. He felt I should have been setting a better example as a captain. He was right, but my thought pattern was like this: *"He is at practice every day and he knows who the best players are. If he chooses to keep them on the bench and causes us to lose, why should I give him*

Influence

my best effort?" He rode me until I reached the boiling point.

I exploded and in my rage blurted out something about how he wasn't using his talent properly. He was shocked by my outburst and issued me an ultimatum: *"I'm the coach. If you don't like it, you can check it in!"* I snatched off my helmet and shoulder pads, threw them to the ground and shouted, *"I'm outta here. I'm not playing for a loser like you!"*

I didn't look back until I reached the locker room, that's when I realized every black player on the team had taken off his equipment and followed me off the field. They were all willing to quit if I was... Whoa! This was back in 1973 the first year of desegregation in the Omaha public school system. Without even trying, I found myself at the head of a movement.

Influence

As we walked past the field on our way home, my eyes locked with the coaches. I could see he was hurt and disappointed. I felt bad too, but he was the one who showed me the door. His actions showed he had no concern for honesty or fair play. Even though I liked him, he lost my respect with his favoritism.

The next day was unbelievable. Word circulated through school that all the black players had boycotted the team and Paul Bryant was the leader. This was the first time I had been recognized for anything other than sports. Things were moving around me so fast that it was impossible to focus. Some of the black students wanted to meet to plan another form of protest, the principal wanted to meet to find out what happened, the coach wanted to meet, parents wanted to meet, my former team mates wanted to meet as well as my white friends. Everyone kept asking me, *"What do you want?"* The walk out wasn't organized; I didn't have an agenda, all I wanted was for the coach to be fair.

Influence

What I didn't know was there were greater issues going on behind the scene. The School Board and the Public School Superintendent had a close eye on Monroe Junior High. Our school was being touted as a model for racial integration. An incident of this nature was totally unacceptable for our principal. The last thing he wanted was for this story to hit the press.

As I understand it, the coach was severely reprimanded by the principal and told to resolve the problem or start looking for a new job. I waited two days before accepting the coach's invitation to meet and as the point-person for the black players I successfully negotiated a truce. A majority of us accepted the coaches offer to come back to the team. Several black players received more playing time and two of them even scored touchdowns.

Looking back, I wonder how that situation could have been handled differently. I actually liked the coach and regret placing him in that position. But he

Influence

was wrong and as a team captain I felt it was my responsibility to act on behalf of my teammates. Hopefully my actions caused him to search his soul and hopefully his future dealings with students were based on fairness, talent and ability rather than skin color.

The boycott of 1973 is what I call it. That single incident positioned me as a leader both on and off the football field. People were willing to follow me; I had influence but didn't have a clue as to how to use it properly. With proper guidance I may have envisioned myself as a leader and maybe I might have accepted responsibility. But like the saying goes, *"If you don't know where you're going, any road will take you there."*

My father died shortly after the football season, my mother worked late and my brother attended college out of town. I had a three-hour window after school to do whatever I wanted. Unlimited freedom allowed me to experiment with drugs, alcohol, sex

Influence

and anything else I desired. I did whatever I wanted and there was no one at home to burst my bubble. I used those three hours of freedom to my advantage and developed a reputation for having a good time. My house became the party spot. After every football game, win or loose, a group of girls would come over my house and meet up with my teammates for an intense kissing session. Everybody kissed everybody -- our reward for on-the-field sacrifice. *Hmmm, maybe that's why those guys followed me off the football field...*

During one of those marathon-kissing sessions, I discovered a tank of Freon in the basement and began to experiment with it. Its effects were like laughing gas. I introduced it to my friends and we forgot all about the kissing. The next thing I knew, kids were coming over the house in droves to try the 'tank.' Every day new faces would show up at my door after school. It became so popular I was considering charging a fee. Isn't it amazing how

189

Influence

quickly destructive behavior can climb through a window of opportunity?

As fate would have it, my brother came home from college and found a gaggle of giggling junior high kids in the house. He discovered the Freon frenzy and decided to call the health department to find out exactly what chemicals were in Freon. Twenty minutes later he rushed in the room, snatched the 'tank' out of my hands and began reading me the riot act. *This stuff can kill you! Freon contains deadly toxins. You are destroying your brain cells every time you take this crap!*

Freon is a liquid/gas refrigerant used to keep air conditioners cool. It's a fairly dangerous substance; individuals who are EPA certified should only handle Freon. In fact, the EPA is fazing out Freon because it is harmful to the environment.

Paranoia engulfed me. I had been messing with Freon on a daily basis for over a week. At least

Influence

forty people had come to my house to try it. How many brain cells could one safely afford to loose? Nightmares of kids dropping dead or suffering permanent brain damage haunted me. I envisioned the media frenzy surrounding the manhunt to find the cause of the Freon epidemic, with every clue leading the authorities closer to me... Surely I would be tagged as the ring leader; the one responsible for influencing his classmates to take deadly gas. I could hear my football coach, *"Paul has always been a bad influence, he persuaded his teammates to quit the team."* There were a few sleepless nights.

I realize how blessed we are that nobody was harmed. I would have been responsible if anything happened to just one my classmates; thank God, no one was injured. The Freon experience was another instance in which people were willing to follow me and I lead them in the wrong direction. It should have caused me to consider the consequences of my actions, but it didn't.

191

Influence

Another memorable influential moment happened one morning before class... I was hanging out before school with my buddies when a young lady I'll call Sugar Baby walked by. I blurted out, *"When are you going to let me get some of that."* I didn't know her very well, and didn't have an attraction to her. I was just showing off in front of my boys. To my surprise, she turned around and said, *"You can get it TONIGHT!"* Dumbfounded and clueless, I didn't know what to say.

I didn't need to say anything because my friend arranged everything. He did such a masterful job of promotion that I will refer to him as, Don King. Don jumped right in and did all the talking; I didn't say a word. He was like an agent. *"OK, where will you meet Paul after school? What time will you be there?"* He set up a rendezvous between Sugar Baby and me at recess.

All day, guys were coming up to me saying things like, *"I heard you and* Sugar Baby *are going to get*

Influence

it on tonight." Embarrassed, but maintaining my cool, I would answer, *"Yeah, man, I'm gonna knock it out."* In reality, I didn't want anything to do with Sugar Baby. I wasn't excited about being with her and I had no intention of keeping that appointment. All day, guys kept coming up to me. They would approach me in gym class, during lunch and in shop class. Don King, had the grapevine working overtime.

I didn't really know or like Sugar Baby. My mouth signed a check I wasn't prepared to cash. At recess, I tried to get away before anyone could see me. As I was exiting the back door, some guys shooting craps behind the building saw me. One of them said, *"Hey Paul, aren't you and Sugar Baby supposed to hook up tonight?"* Thinking quickly, I said, *"Yeah, I'm checking the back to make sure she isn't trying to sneak away, because I'm going to knock the bottom out."* Another crapshooter spoke up, *"She's supposed to be waiting at the front of the school. Let's go see if she is there."* Damn! I

Influence

couldn't believe it! The crapshooters busted me. The crapshooters! If these guys knew what was going on, the whole school knew.

Several of the biggest losers in the school escorted me through the building. This clandestine event had linked me with people I never associated with. When we arrived at the front of the school, Sugar Baby was there just like she said. And so were Don King and about eight other guys. I asked Sugar Baby if she was ready to go. She said yes, and we began the seven-block walk to my house.

Don King and his band of idiots followed about twenty yards behind us. If that wasn't bad enough, they were making loud sounds and noises. The grunts and groans I assumed someone makes when he's "knockin' the bottom out." *"Uh, Ummm, Ohhh!"*

That was one of the longest walks of my life. Seven blocks with someone I wasn't attracted to, really didn't know, on a mission to do something I didn't want to do; with nine fools following behind step for step making catcalls. The power of peer pressure is amazing; every step I wanted to stop and rain on the parade; but for some reason I couldn't, I felt an obligation to follow through.

When we reached my house, Sugar Baby and I left Don King and his cronies standing in the driveway. I led Sugar Baby to my bedroom, and she pushed me out. I assumed she had second thoughts, which was all right with me because I was looking for a way out. Now I could tell everyone she chickened out because she knew, *"I was going to knock the bottom out."* I went to the kitchen, made a peanut butter and jelly sandwich and walked over to the window to wave at the guys who were now sitting on my front porch. The number of fools had dwindled to three.

Sugar Baby unlocked my bedroom door and said, *"Come on, I'm ready."* I walked in the room, and

195

she was naked except for one of my tank top T-shirts. Without saying a word, I unzipped my pants, got on top of her and did what came natural. No kissing. No foreplay. Just mount up and ride... It was bad. It was really bad! I remember her breathing sporadically, pulling at my face saying, *"Kiss me, kiss me,"* as I strained my neck pulling away not to kiss her. I had peanut butter and jelly breath, I was fully dressed, it was definitely not the portrait of intimacy. I was thinking, *"Is this what everyone is so crazy about? Is this it? There has to be more to it than this?"* Then unexpectedly that magical moment hit my system. I discovered what the hubbub was all about. As if I were being electrocuted, every nerve in my body, from my forehead to my toes, quivered uncontrollably. My muscles were doing things I could not control. I didn't know what was happening, but I liked it. After my seizure of pleasure I got up without saying a word, immediately went to the front door and told the guys, *"I killed it! I killed it!"* The guys gave me

Influence

high-fives; they looked at me with disbelief and sheer admiration. I was "The Man!"

I was on the porch lying about the details when out comes Sugar Baby dressed and ready to go.

She immediately stole my thunder. Sugar Baby was the center of attention and she totally enjoyed the stage. She was the Queen Bee surrounded by drones' eagerly positioning themselves for her next visit. She teased and encouraged them. I didn't understand how she could flirt with them after just being with me. Suddenly, it occurred to me, Sugar Baby had just notched her belt! She was the one who *"knocked the bottom out,"* not me. As far as I was concerned we couldn't walk her home fast enough. This is the pitiful story of how I lost my virginity...

Once again I had used my influence to lead someone down the wrong path, however this time I did it to myself. The 5 seconds of pleasure was not

Influence

worth what I lost. I often wonder what my adolescent years would have been like if my first intimate experience was with someone I cared about, someone I loved.

I had numerous internal debates over including this story or not. I vacillated back and forth concerning how much of my personal life I should share. My decision fell on the side of full disclosure because every young person in our society, no matter where they live or what their social or economic background, will confront the decision of when to become sexually active. Just maybe my story will empower someone to think before they act.

The truth is, I was an immature boy searching for his manhood. Sexual conquests were adult actions that allowed me to communicate with older, mature boys. I seemed to move up the proverbial status pole with the telling of each exploit. I was really a goofy teenager who preferred hanging with his

Influence

buddies and playing sports. I stopped being myself to gain the approval of others.

Sex became my ultimate quest. There was only one thing on my mind. I was so focused on getting girls into bed that I never explored their personalities. Many decent girls were hurt by my stupidity. Unfortunately, young men don't think while they are sowing their oats, I know. Boys will say and do just about anything to get what they want. Once their mission is accomplished, it's 'Bye, Bye' and they move on to the next adventure. They don't understand that taking something so special and reducing it to an accomplishment – like scoring a touchdown or sinking a put – minimizes the experience. And once you take something down from the pedestal, it becomes extremely difficult to put it back.

Sadly it's the young women who most often get hurt in these relationships. By nature, females are looking for loving relationships and males are looking for sex. Many women are adapting the same attitudes as men, but it's not natural and in the long run it will be detrimental. Sex is being mistaken for love. The warped mindset necessary to maintain multiple unattached intimate relationships will affect a mother's ability to nurture her children. It will be very difficult to give love if you don't know love yourself.

It is inexcusably complicated for kids today. They are bombarded with sexual images on Prime Time Television, Commercials, Videos, Music and even Cartoons. SEX SELLS! Everything in society pushes children toward promiscuity, the current fashions, and unfiltered communications via cell phones, text mail and the Internet. Take a moment and observe the sexuality of the role models the media choose to highlight. Unfortunately, what they see is what they will be.

I'm still repentant. It's quite obvious to me now how wrong and damaging my behavior was. The

Influence

sad reality is that I can't change the past. I have no way to wipe the slate clean. I wish there was a way to make amends with every young lady who unknowingly wandered onto my path and became road-kill along my highway to enlightenment. I realize I folded to the forces of peer pressure. Given a second chance, I would not have taken Sugar Baby home...

This is one of the many reasons I thank God for salvation through Jesus Christ. Without this belief my conscious would deteriorate my mind. I will share this story with my children. I hope it will encourage them to abstain until they are married. What's that saying? *"A smart man will learn from his mistakes; a wise man will learn from the mistakes of others, and a fool, a fool will never learn."*

I hope my influence on children is as strong today as it was on my classmates in Junior High School. Through the Wesley House Leadership Academy I

201

Influence

am once again trying to Influence middle school children. My mission is to nurture and develop future leaders.

The mother of one of the students in the Academy called one morning and said, *"Mr. Bryant, I want you to know what an influence you are on my son. I was driving him to school this morning and he asked me; 'Mom, how much money do I have in the bank? I asked him. Why? He responded, I think I can be a millionaire by the time I graduate from college. Warren Buffett started with 1 dollar and he is a billionaire. I have more money than him, if I increase my net worth every year, I can be a millionaire. Mr. Bryant, for my fourth grade son to be talking about his net worth and even thinking about how to become rich is because of your influence."*

Her son was a student in the Junior Executives program that I teach. Junior Executives are 10 –13 year old students who learn the basics of business

Influence

analysis and accounting. The following is one of my favorite stories.

I took a group of Junior Executives to tour the headquarters of the Union Pacific Railroad Company. My students were well prepared with their blue blazers and khakis slacks. They looked everyone in the eye, giving firm handshakes, just as they had been taught. There was a buzz going through the office about these well-behaved young people who looked so great in their clothes.

We toured the entire office and now it was time to meet with the CEO, Dick Davidson. We were in the executive boardroom on the top floor of their new facility. By Dick's presentation, I assumed he must have had a very successful day. He was animated, on his feet, making a very colorful presentation. He had no problem holding the attention of my 4th, 5th and 6th grade students. He told them about his thirty-one years with the railroad and how working hard and avoiding trouble had enabled him to start his career as a brakeman and move into the top position.

He told the students, *"One of the things I've found is that leaders always gravitate to the front of the room. You see this chair? One of my board members used to sit right here; close to the fire!"* *He had to resign a while ago to accept a position with the government. He left my board to become the Vice President of the United States. "*

The kids started whispering amongst themselves, *"The Vice President? Wow! The Vice President was in this room?"* Looking pretty confident seeing his comments receive the desired effect, he said, *"That's right, Dick Cheney sat on my board."* He grabbed his belt, hiked up his pants and said, *"Any questions?"*

The hand of seven-year-old Brice immediately shot into the air; Dick pointed at him and said, *"Yes young man?"* Brice said, *"Mr. Davidson, what*

Influence

were the revenues for Union Pacific last year?"
The expression on his face was priceless. Dick
looked at me and said, *"Paul, what are you
teaching these kids? That's a great question, young
man; the revenues for the Union Pacific
Corporation were 46 Billion dollars last year."*
Again, the kids were in awe, *"Billion? Did he say
billion? Wow!"* Then one of the kids blurted out,
*"We were at KETV last week and they only had 50
million in revenues!"*

My young protégés were shining. It was show time,
and they bought their 'A' game. The expression on
my face had to be the epitome of pride. These were
inner city children; the majority of them are from
single parent, low-income families. They were
sitting comfortably in the executive conference
room of a Fortune 500 company having a
conversation with the CEO about revenues and net
income. And they knew what they were talking
about...

Influence

Influence is the ability to inspire others to act. At the end of the day, my effectiveness will be measured by the impact my students have on society. What kind of influence do you have and how are you using it? 360 Degrees of influence means you affect people below, beside and above you.

MONROE JUNIOR HIGH 1972 FOOTBALL TEAM

UNION PACIFIC WELCOMES

WESLEY HOUSE
ACADEMY

Chapter Eleven

Legacy Leaving Leaders

How many do you know?

Have you ever met someone who makes a lasting impression on you with nothing more than the power of their personality? Someone whose life embodies the mathematical equation for Purpose Living Leadership, $(VP + CP) \div (F \times H) = I$. If you have, then you've probably met a Purpose Living Leader? Much too often we don't recognize the impact these people have on our lives until they are gone. Only then do we appreciate the privilege we had to walk with them down destiny's path.

I've been blessed to know and work with several Purpose Living Leaders. Three of them, however, stand taller than the rest because they helped shape

Legacy Leaving Leaders

and mold my character. They were contributors on my trek to find purpose. The time I spent with them was meaningful; their memories help me to see the significance of my journey…

The first is Don Clifton, the former Chairman of The Gallup Organization and the founder of Selection Research Inc. Don was an incredible man with the ability to touch and influence everyone he came in contact with. He served as my mentor, teacher, advisor and coach. I will never forget the day we met.

I spent several hours being interviewed by executives within The Gallup Organization. This was the final dance, where you meet the decision makers of an organization for them to determine if they want you on their team. Without exception, everyone I met talked with reverence about their Chairman, Don Clifton, a researcher in his seventies, who consistently put in forty-hour weeks.

209

Legacy Leaving Leaders

As fate would have it, the last person on my schedule was on a conference call, so I waited outside of his office. As I walked the floor admiring the décor; I noticed Don's name plate over one of the doors. I walked over to look in his office and to my surprise he was sitting at his desk. He looked up and asked, *"May I help you?"* The ensuing conversation changed my life.

I said, *"Mr. Clifton, my name is Paul Bryant and I am interviewing for a position with your company. Everyone I meet is in awe of you. You truly have the respect of your team. Would you mind answering a question for me? What is it about this company that causes a seasoned gentleman like you to spend so much time at the office? You have made your fortune you could be doing anything you want at this stage of your life."*

Don said, *"I come in every day because I'm on a mission to advance "strengths science" to help the whole world know their strengths. One of the*

210

Legacy Leaving Leaders

purposes of the Gallup Organization is to promote democracy around the world. You see, in some countries people are not allowed to voice their opinions. If you are not free to say what you think, you can kiss the all the other liberties goodbye. Our opinion polls give people a voice, a chance to be heard. My goal is for the Gallup Organization to be the first company to win the Nobel Peace Prize."

He paused and our eyes locked. I looked deep into his intense blue pupils and could see he was dead serious. It made the hairs on the back of my neck stand up. For ten years I had been a banker; my only goals were to help the company surpass the previous year's earnings. The prospect of working to promote democracy was foreign to me. The idea of utilizing my talents to win a Nobel Peace Prize was exhilarating. I immediately knew I wanted to work with him. We talked for about an hour and when I finally exited his office I said, *"I'm looking forward to helping you win the Nobel Prize."*

Legacy Leaving Leaders

Six months after accepting their offer I was promoted to Vice President. For the next five years Don and I worked closely, our offices were 15 steps apart.

I will never forget the meeting with my first client, the Mayor of Lincoln, Mike Johanns. Mike later became the Governor of Nebraska, then the Secretary of Agriculture and is currently projected to be Nebraska's next U.S. Senator.

We were in the executive board room with the Mayor, Police Chief, and several of Johanns' direct reports. The small talk ended and it was time to deliver the results of our research. It was time for the Chairman to do his thing; I was looking forward to observing the master at work. This was our first time presenting to a paying customer. Without warning, Don turned to me and said, *"Paul, you make the presentation."*

Legacy Leaving Leaders

There was no time to debate, it was show time and all eyes were on me. Did I prepare to deliver the technical piece of that presentation, NO! Did I handle the situation, YES! Am I now comfortable making impromptu presentations, ABSOLUTELY! Experience can be the best teacher. This was a real-time training program Don frequently used that I titled, "Sink or Swim..."

Over the next five years Don and I traveled the country from Harvard to Hawaii making presentations and business calls. Don not only showed me I could swim; he gave me the opportunity to fly.

We conducted a national study for the 100 Black Men of America on The Miracles of Mentoring. During the Press Conference at the national release of the results, Don said to me, *"A mentor is someone who sits on your shoulder and whispers in your ear, even when they are no longer around."*

213

Legacy Leaving Leaders

It's been close to a decade since Don past and I can still hear his voice…

Another Purpose Living Leader I had the privilege to know and work with was my good friend, Steve Hogan, the founder and Executive Director of the Hogan's Heroes Golf Program. Steve was the first African-American PGA professional in the State of Nebraska and was nationally recognized. The PGA of America and USA Kids Golf named him the National Junior Golf Leader of the Year and One of the Top 50 Golf Teachers in the country. For the past four years Steve had taught the children in my academy how to play the game of golf.

Steve's funeral was November 29, 2008; it was the most beautiful home going I've ever attended. The church was packed; The Mayor, Congressman and City Council representatives all paid their respects. Videos of his life and choir selections tugged at everyone's heartstrings. There were numerous stories of how Steve had touched someone's life

Legacy Leaving Leaders

and many people spoke of the need to continue his legacy. A unified feeling throughout the church was that our community had lost someone special.

The defining moment came when his son, Steven Hogan II, made the final statement for the family. I sat in awe as Little Steve added the exclamation point to his father's funeral. This had to be the most difficult presentation of his life and he nailed it! His poise, articulation and delivery were incredible.

My mind raced over thoughts of seeing Big and Little Steve together on the golf course and the times Big Steve would boast of Little Steve's accomplishments, which were many. Little Steve graduated from college, he excelled on both debate and golf teams and he held a leadership position with the Obama campaign in Minnesota.

Steve was one of the few people I told about this book. He encouraged me to stay on task and I needled him about writing his own book. We were

215

Legacy Leaving Leaders

both native Omahans' with dreams of making our community better.

I remembered a verse in the Bible; Proverbs 10:7 that says, *"The memory of the righteous will be a blessing."* And then it occurred to me, Steve's legacy was standing at the microphone. His son was the embodiment of all the great words that were being said. The best of Steve Hogan will live on through his son, his daughter, and the many children he touched through his program. There was a tingling sensation on the back of my neck; a feeling I often get when experiencing a spiritual encounter. I wiped a tear, took a deep sigh and thought, *"What a Great legacy, there is no better way to leave this earth!"* Steve Hogan was a Purpose Living Leader.

Don and Steve made an impact on my life. Knowing them motivated me to reach for a higher level. They inspired me to find purpose in my life. The bible says, *"Iron will sharpen iron and a man will sharpen the continence of his friend."* I

216

Legacy Leaving Leaders

consider it an honor for them to have called me, friend.

However, the most influential Purpose Living Leader in my life has been Mildred D. Brown, the Founder, Owner, Editor and Publisher of the Omaha Star Newspaper. Aunt Millie was a fireball. Her grit, determination and willpower were second to none. She was the epitome of self determination. Mildred Brown founded the Omaha Star in 1938; During a time when America was not accepting of either Blacks or Women she started a newspaper and never missed a publication.

I frequently ate dinner with her in her private office and listened as she lobbied politicians and business leaders for various causes. She was a dedicated, persistent, behind-the–scenes activist, who exerted an extreme amount of influence from the telephone in that back office.

Legacy Leaving Leaders

When she wasn't selling advertisements or promoting a cause, she would pull out old photo albums and share with me the stories behind the pictures. I was fascinated by the role of the press in the civil rights movement. She had pictures in the Oval Office of the White House with different presidents; pictures with Martin Luther King, Jesse Jackson, Whitney Young, Ralph Abernathy and many, many others. She had relationships with major national leaders and had the pictures to prove it. In most of those pictures, she was the only woman in the room.

She was inducted into the Omaha Business Hall of Fame and had received almost every award possible. There were well over a hundred plaques in her office. Aunt Millie was a powerful person and for some reason, she took me under her wing. She would invite me to elaborate events and introduce me to people as her Son; I couldn't take that title away from my mother, so she became Aunt Millie. Her invitations opened doors I didn't know existed.

Legacy Leaving Leaders

Our relationship is the result of a unique circumstance... I was a graduate student in my mid twenties working an internship with the InterNorth Corporation. I worked for one of the highest ranking African American Executives in the city.

He was an excellent boss, roll model and a fantastic mentor. His departure from the company was swift, quiet and unexpected. No one in the company would discuss the reason for his leaving and as an intern; I was in no position to pry.

His exit happened days before the culmination of my first project, The Newcomer Reception. I was tasked with organizing a major reception for African American's who had recently relocated to the city. The event was a collaborative effort with other major employers and social service organizations. It was a huge success with well over 500 people in attendance...

219

Legacy Leaving Leaders

After the affair the photographer delivered the proofs for me to select which pictures I wanted to go into the paper. I showed them to my new boss and he told me not to put any pictures of my mentor in the paper. The Newcomers reception was my mentor's idea; I was already frustrated because of his unknown departure. I wasn't stupid; without him I wouldn't have been hired. The suggestion to 'strike his name from the record,' irritated me.

I took the proofs to the Omaha Star and asked to speak with Mrs. Brown; this was my first conversation with her. I asked if we could speak in private and I told her my dilemma. I reminded her that the pictures were taken by her photographer, so actually they were hers to do with as she wished. She said, *"This is my paper and I'll put whoever I want in it! What's your name again, boy, I like you; you've got fight. You tell your boss you returned the pictures to me with his recommendations. I'll handle the rest."*

Legacy Leaving Leaders

The Newcomer Reception was the front page lead story on the next edition of the Star. For the first time ever, a full page pictorial was dedicated to an event. Several pictures of my mentor were prominently placed with a large photo of him in the center of the pictorial.

That was the beginning of my friendship with Mildred D. Brown. I truly loved 'Aunt Millie' and I miss the late night dinners and history lessons in her back office. One of the greatest honors I've received was the opportunity to serve as the Master of Ceremonies for the inauguration of the Mildred Brown strolling park and the unveiling of a bronze statue of her.

Each of these people touched my life. Much of the wisdom I gleaned from them I am passing on to my children. I dedicate this book to their memories may they never be forgotten...

Legacy Leaving Leaders

An old friend would say, *"You should give someone their flowers while they are living."* This means you shouldn't wait until someone's funeral to say good things about them. If they've done something worthy of a compliment, give it to them while they can appreciate it.

If you are blessed to be traveling life's road with a Purpose Living Leader, take some time and let them know you are enjoying the ride.

~ Donald O. Clifton ~

Mike Johanns, Don & Patrick V. Murphy

Kickin' it with Don and Robin in Hawaii...

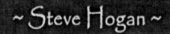

~ Steve Hogan ~

Steve and I with a young golfer...

Steve Hogan Sr. & Jr. Share a Teaching Moment...

~ Mildred D. Brown ~

Nate Goldston, President Gourmet Foods
Alvin Goodwin, President Omaha Economic Development Corporation
Earl Graves, Founder & Publisher of Black Enterprises Magazine

Chapter Twelve

Destiny

Are you where you're supposed to be?

There are times in life when circumstances appear ordained to happen. Some folk say these situations are mere coincidence; others call them fate. I believe they are Gods way of steering us toward our destiny.

> *"Standing in the right place at the right time; the stars align perfectly and due to no effort of your own, miraculous things occur."*
>
> *- Paul Bryant*

When I look to the origin of my networking prowess, one incident stands out like a pimple on the prom queen. I was a 25-year-old graduate student with an internship with the Enron

Destiny

Corporation. I worked for Bob Armstrong, one of the highest-ranking black executives in the city.

Bob was a visionary and a great mentor. He introduced me to the corporate lifestyle and allowed me to accompany him to Chicago for the annual convention of the National Association of Market Developers (NAMD). The membership of NAMD consisted of the crème de la crème of African American marketing executives. Well-established members included individuals like H. Naylor Fitzhugh, the first black graduate of the Harvard Business School and the first black Vice President of the Pepsi Cola Company.

The opening reception for the conference was held in the atrium of a museum on Lakeshore Drive. It was a first-class event by any standard. Several people in the room were regulars in Jet and Ebony magazines. Most were in the 40–50 age range and appeared very secure in their careers. I was a self-

227

Destiny

conscious 25-year-old kid from Omaha, Nebraska on his first trip to the big city.

Feeling totally out of place, I stood alone at the buffet table with a shrimp in one hand and Chablis in the other. Fully engaged in an internal conversation, I asked, *"What will I talk to these people about? I'm only an intern. I don't belong here. God, how will I fit in?"*

Suddenly, there was a rush toward the front door -- The kind of commotion seen when a hoard of teenage fans are clamoring to get a glimpse of their idols. Everyone in the room was moving in the same direction. Spotlights from mobile news cameras were flashing back and forth across the ceiling. The echo of hundreds of shoe heels clicking on the marble floor combined with the murmuring of the crowd added to the excitement. I was very curious as to what was going on, but my grandfather's words burned in my ears, *"Never be*

Destiny

one to run after a crowd." So I held my position and watched with anticipation.

Suddenly the reason for the commotion strutted through the door. It was Chicago's Mayor, Harold Washington. Everyone was in awe of Mayor Washington. He was the Barack Obama of the eighties. He was one of the first African Americans elected to run a major city. He stepped through the crowd with the presence of a celebrity. The people parted like he was Moses walking through the Red Sea. He walked as stately and dignified as I had ever seen a man walk. His chin was high and his shoulders were straight. He looked neither left nor right. He strolled through the crowd never stopping, never pausing to acknowledge anyone.

"Mayor Washington, Mayor Washington," they called. He marched directly over to the buffet table. Walked right up to me, held out his hand and said, *"Hi, I'm Harold Washington."* I tossed the shrimp, held out my hand and said, *"Paul, Paul Bryant."*

229

Destiny

The crowd encircled us and a photographer said, *"Let me get a picture."* Mayor Washington paused for one picture. Then he and his entourage disappeared on an elevator. The other individuals in the photograph were LeBaron Taylor, Vice President of Sony, Eugene McCullers, Vice President of Coca Cola Company and Al Curtis Robinson, Vice President of Mutual of Omaha. That picture made its way into several newspapers and a national magazine.

For some reason, Mayor Washington walked through a crowd of people directly over to me and introduced himself. People in the crowd now perceived me to be someone of importance. And who was I to tell them any different. I no longer had to worry about starting conversations because people were approaching me to find out who I was.

The most memorable person in the room was Vernita Harris, a model from Houston Texas. She had just been selected to represent Dark and Lovely

Destiny

hair care products. Not only did Vernita possess good looks, she had a Masters in Business Administration and a mind for business. She quickly became my newest best friend. I closely observed her finesse and big-city attitude. She was able to do the simplest things with flair. Her ability to hail taxis, select wine, order from the menu and glean information from men was amazing! Most guys fell for her charm, and she positioned me as a direct beneficiary of their kindness. Because of Vernita Harris, I gained immediate access to the "In Crowd."

We had velvet rope access and un-carded entree to the VIP parties. From that conference forward, I've viewed myself as an A-list individual. As I look back I can't help but feel blessed at the access I've attained. I always believed there was a reason for those experiences and felt compelled to catalogue them.

Destiny

One of the highlights of my professional career has been the opportunity to interact and develop relationships with interesting people from a variety of different backgrounds. There was a time in my life when I traveled at a faster pace and ran in different circles. I'll share some of these experiences not to impress you but to make you aware of who I am and where I've been. I feel very blessed to have had these experiences; which are astonishing to me because I live in a city not exactly known for its sizzle or pizzazz.

I've been the recipient of political appointments and directorships on various boards. I'd eaten dinner with President Bill Clinton, lunch with Gen. Colin Powell, Thanksgiving dinner at the home of Dr. Maya Angelou and toasted cocktails with former Secretary of State Henry Kissinger. I was a guest on a seven day cruise with talk show queen Oprah Winfrey, spent the 4th of July at the estate of award-winning songwriters Nick Ashford and Valerie Simpson, spent a day at home with Heavyweight

Destiny

Boxing Champion, Evander Holyfield and spent a night aboard a Trident Nuclear Submarine in the middle of the Pacific Ocean.

I've held receptions for Stedman Graham, NBA All Star Allan Houston, Best Selling Author George Fraser and my children have hosted a sleep over for the son and daughter of Grammy winning gospel singer BeBe Winans. I've made an impromptu presentation to more than 300 police chiefs and visited Africa at the invitation of Forbes list Billionaire Shake Muhammad Al-Amoudi, the wealthiest person of African decent on this planet. I once walked the red carpet of a movie premiere with paparazzi and screaming fans, attended the Essence Awards in New York with a fourth row center section seat directly in front of Janet Jackson and I've sat in the front row for a Bishop T.D. Jakes sermon.

I've held a conversation with Bishop Desmond Tutu and I cold called Gale Sayers and convinced him to

233

Destiny

host my golf tournament. I've met dozens of professional athletes including Hall of Fame inductees: Michael Jordon, Charles Barkley, Ernie Banks, Bob Gibson, Paul Horning, Kellen Winslow and John Elway. I once walked up to Basketball Stars Julius Erving and Isiah Thomas, introduced myself and ultimately walked away with a $400,000 contract.

I spent 15 hours with Lee Brown on that historic day when he was elected the first black Mayor of Houston, Texas and I've met with the Mayors of the ten largest cities in America, in their offices.

Yeah, I've been blessed to have had encounters with successful people at the height of their careers. What stood out most about them was their level of engagement in life. These people used their talents and abilities to the fullest; they had purpose. It wasn't about the money, fame or notoriety; it was about the work. They were full participants in the

Destiny

game of life because everyday they put it all on the table.

Are you simply going through the motions on your job, with your family, in your community? Has life become a mundane routine that has you living for the weekends? Ask yourself these questions. Are you are fulfilling your purpose; are you doing that 'thing' you were put on earth to do? Each of us has something we can do better than anyone on this planet. My interaction with successful people has shown me that true fulfillment comes when you identify your talent; recognize your purpose and then persistently pursue that purpose with passion.

In an earlier chapter I shared the story of being overcome with the motivation to write as a passenger aboard a plane leaving Phoenix, Arizona. Is it a coincidence or destiny that I am writing the final chapter of this Book in Phoenix?

Destiny

I haven't been back to Phoenix since 2001 and my purpose for being here couldn't be more diametrically apposed. Seven years ago I was a Councilor in a civic organization named the Knights of Ak-Sar-Ben. Our retreat, masked under the guise of social service, was really a vacation get away for about 20 businessmen from my community.

Today, I am one of 150 non-profit executives attending a fundraising conference sponsored by the United Methodist Church. We are learning about creative, cutting edge methods to raise money online. In the midst of our nation's economic crisis the survival of many nonprofit agencies depends on our ability to attract new sources of funding. This is definitely no vacation.

Not only are my reasons for being in Phoenix complete opposites, but also the focus of my writing is poles apart. The original concept was an autobiographical piece that chronicled my experiences growing up in the 'hood'. I was like an

Destiny

urban Huckleberry Finn navigating the backstreets to eventually reach the boardroom. At one point I thought it was finished, but for some reason I wasn't comfortable getting it published. After several revisions, again I felt the book was complete. This time the focus was perseverance. My plan was to use my life stories to inspire young people to overcome obstacles and persevere through hardships. I don't know why, but that version didn't feel right either.

By this time, The Book, as it was referred to in my household, had became a source of contention. I would carve out significant periods of time and hibernate when I felt motivated to write. This didn't sit well with my wife, Robin, who did more than her share of housework and child rearing.

She found it hard to support The Book project after twice hearing me boast about being finished, only to announce later that something didn't feel right before putting the assignment away. It was difficult for her to understand how I could log off the computer and discontinue discussion about the book for months, even years at a time.

But now, the time is perfect! This era is like none other in the history of America. Never before has Leadership captured the attention of the world more than during the U.S. presidential election of 2008. Purpose Living Leadership is an idea whose time has come.

Something about Barack Obama gives people hope. He is able to touch people's emotions. More tears were shed during his victory than in any other presidential election in history. Without serving one day in office he has restored our collective faith in the goodness of our country. Even the most faithful Republican in the reddest state would have to agree that even though Obama will enter office with more challenges than any other President in history; everything is in his favor to create one of the greatest Presidential Legacies of all time.

Destiny

But let's get back to Phoenix. What an exotic place with its majestic mountains and sequoia cactuses. Just the name, Phoenix, conjures up thoughts of the mythical bird that rises from the ashes. What a metaphorical twist it would be to begin and end The Book in Phoenix. I was a man on a mission; my intention was to spend every spare moment during the conference in my room writing. I left home proclaiming to my wife and children, *"When I return, The Book will be finished!"*

I was ticked off when I checked into the hotel and discovered I would have two roommates. The Methodist Church sponsored the conference and they handled all of the arrangements. I wanted solitude and didn't feel like being social. A couple of lunches, a dinner or two and I'd be headed home with an unfinished book. The last thing I wanted to see was that look of doubt from my family again.

It has been said that God works in mysterious ways. Destiny is the only word I can think of to describe

239

Destiny

the next few days. I was in Phoenix just to meet my roommates. They were like angels sent to show me the purpose for writing this book. Two complete strangers showed me the reason for giving my thoughts to the world.

My roommates were Lurone Jennings and Bill Holland, the Executive Director and Business Manager for the United Methodist Neighborhood Center in Chattanooga Tennessee. Lurone was the founder of an organization named, The V Team Leadership Network, which stands for Voices with a Vision for Victory in the Game of Life. The mission of the V Team is to change history by accelerating the spread of the Gospel through leaders empowered by the Holy Spirit. They are mobilizing and training a network of urban leaders to teach other leaders how to share the Gospel of Jesus Christ. The V Team is an affiliate of the International Leadership Institute and uses their Eight Core Values of Christian Leadership to teach urban leaders. The Eight Core Values are the

Destiny

product of an International Leadership Institute global study of faith-based leaders.

I was stunned after reading their Eight Core Values; these were the same principles being taught to the students in the Wesley House Leadership Academy! The International Leadership Institute identified, organized and defined them. They also developed work sheets and questions around them, but they were the same ideals being taught to the youth in my academy.

I scrapped my plans to hibernate and dived into their material. I finished reading their training booklet and brochure from cover to cover in one day. Lurone and I were kindred souls; he had written a book titled, "The Crisis in Urban America" and my Masters Degrees are in Urban Studies and Urban Education. We both shared an equal passion for improving Urban Communities.

241

Destiny

During the evenings I tried to seclude myself and carve out time to work on the book. But there was always a knock on the door; Lurone would poke his head in the room and we would end up talking for hours. I didn't mind at all. He turned out to be the mentor I didn't know I needed. His wisdom and knowledge assured me the time was right to finish this book. He told me, *"Paul, you have a responsibility to release this book to the world."*

Lurone was very open to adding me to the V Team so that I could teach the Eight Core Values. Having those values gave their program authenticity and credibility. I thought about how similar they were to what I was teaching and I wondered why I hadn't taken the time to create a curriculum.

I lay in bed contemplating how to mesh the Eight Core Values together with the Wesley House Leadership Academy. Somewhat envious at how much further the V Team had progressed than my Leadership Academy. I suddenly thought of a story

Destiny

I had read in Dr. Dennis Kimbro's book, Think and Grow Rich, A Black Choice.

In his introduction Dr. Kimbro says, *"Black Americans who seek a way to abandon a mediocre life, a start on the grand highway to success – here is your road map!*

This map is not new. It was developed just after the Civil War in the form of a lecture entitled "Acres of Diamonds" by a lawyer and newspaper editor named Russell H. Conwell. In 1881, Dr. Conwell also became a minister, and it was in this role that he developed his talk, which he delivered some 8000 times to audiences across the country. These appearances earned him nearly $8 million in lecture fees, which he used to found Temple University in Philadelphia, Pennsylvania, to serve "poor and deserving young men."

"Acres of Diamonds" was the true story of a poor farmer who settled in Africa and spent years

243

Destiny

struggling to raise his crops. His land was rocky and difficult to till. Disenfranchised with his circumstances, the farmer became increasingly fascinated by tales of "easy wealth" gained by men who had searched for and discovered diamonds in the countryside. He, too, wanted to be rich. He grew tired of the endless labor, and impulsively sold his farm to search for diamonds. For the rest of his life he wandered the vast African continent searching for the gleaming gems. But the great discovery always eluded him. Finally, in a fit of despondency, broken financially, spiritually, and emotionally, he threw himself into a river and drowned.

Meanwhile, the man who had bought his farm found a rather large and unusual stone in a stream that cut through his property. It turned out to be a diamond of enormous value. Stunned by his newfound wealth, the farmer discovered that his land was virtually covered with such stones. It was

Destiny

---

to become one of the world's richest diamond mines!

Now, the first farmer had unknowingly owned acres of diamonds. He sold the property for practically nothing in order to look for riches elsewhere. If only he had taken the time to study and realize what diamonds looked like in their rough state, and had first thoroughly explored the land he had owned, he would have found the riches he sought – on the very land he had been living upon!

What so profoundly affected Dr. Conwell, and subsequently thousands of others who heard this lecture, was the fact that each of us, at any given moment, is standing in the middle of his or her own acre of diamonds. If only we acquire the wisdom and patience to intelligently and effectively examine our circumstances and to explore the work in which we are now engaged, we usually will find that it contains the riches we seek – whether they be material, spiritual, or both.

Destiny

Before we go running off to what we think are greener pastures, let's make sure that our own is not just as green, or perhaps even greener! Oftentimes, while we're looking at other pastures, other people are busy looking at ours. There's nothing more pitiful than the person who wastes his or her life wandering from one thing to another, like the improvident seeker of diamonds, forever looking for the pot of gold at the end of the rainbow and never staying with one thing long enough to find it. For no matter what your goal may be, or whatever form your riches may take, you can be sure that your start on the road to its attainment can be found somewhere within your present surroundings."

I thought about Dr. Kimbro's words and remembered the first thing I created after accepting the Executive Director position, the Wesley House Creed. I sat in a conference room at the Leadership Institute for Urban Education and asked God for a theme. I wanted a slogan to describe the Wesley House mission and explain the new vision. I

Destiny

walked over to the black board, picked up a piece of chalk and wrote this Creed on the first take.

"We believe in God.
We have faith that he will empower us to overcome any obstacles and persevere any hardships.
Through self-discipline we will grow into adults of honor and integrity.
Our legacy will be a source of pride to our family and community. "

Every student in the Academy has to learn the Creed within his or her first week in the program. It is recited often; multiple times a day. It is a teaching tool we use when directing and correcting behavior. The 12 Principals of a Purpose Living Leader have been sitting under my nose since May of 2005.

1. Belief in God
2. Faith
3. Empowerment
4. Overcoming Obstacles
5. Persevering Hardships
6. Self Discipline
7. Honor

Destiny

8. Integrity
9. Legacy
10. Pride
11. Family
12. Community

The Leadership Institute for Urban Education is developing a Leadership Curriculum that will incorporate the 12 Principals of a Purpose Living Leader. These innovative new ideas will be piloted at the Wesley House Leadership Academy.

Destiny brought me to Phoenix and introduced me to Lurone Jennings and Bill Holland. They caused me to see how green the grass was in my own back yard.

What are you looking past? Is there a diamond field you are over looking in your back yard? Take a moment to inventory the blessings around you. I call them blessings because we have a tendency to take them for granted. If you don't agree, imagine what your life would be like without them...

My National debut with LaBaron Taylor, Eugene McCullers, Mayor Harold Washington, & Al Robinson

The unforgetable, Vernita Harris...

Legendary business icon, H. Naylor Fitzhugh...

Bill Clinton, Henry Kissinger & Colin Powell

Alec Gallup
of the
Gallup Organization

Casper Weinberger,
Former Sec. of Defense

Lee Brown, the night
he became the 1st black
Mayor of Houston

Mohammed Al Amoudi
ranked 43rd richest person in
the World by Forbes magazine
in 2009

Stedman, Oprah,
& Robin in the
Florida Keys

Martin Luther King, III
at unveiling of
MLK Jr. Statue

Legacy Leaving Leaders...

C. Delores Tucker, founder
of the National Congress of
Black Women and the
Bethune-DuBois Institute

Dr. Dorthory Height, Chair
and President Emerita -
National Council of Negro
Women, Congressional
Medal of Honor Awardee

Maya Angelou is an accomplished poet,
an award winning writer, a journalist,
an activist, a performer, a dancer,
an actress, a director and a teacher

Nebraska's Finest...

Ron Brown, Nathaniel Goldston,
Johnny Rodgers and Tom Osborne

Best Selling Authors

George Fraser

Dennis Kimbro

Paul Bryant, vice president of the Gallup Organization, introduces guest speaker Dr. Dennis Kimbro (right) to young black achievers at the DoubleTree Hotel. "Find your area of excellence," Kimbro said, "and pour your whole heart and soul in to it."

Dr. Michael Eric Dyson

Kickin' it with Dr. J and Ron Boone

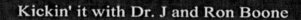

Pro Golfer Tina Mickelson & Former N.Y. Knick Allan Houston

Chapter Thirteen

Values

What do you believe?

We were sitting in our favorite booth at Lonelle's one Sunday, when a Preacher walked over to our table. Lonell's is my family's favorite Soul Food restaurant; it's a popular after church breakfast stop. *"Good Afternoon Brother Bryant, Mrs. Bryant. You certainly have a beautiful family. Yes indeed, you are a fine looking family. You look like the Obama's, Brother Bryant!"*

I'm sure the large color photo of the first family on the front page of the newspaper had something to do with his comments. Nevertheless his statement was a compliment of the highest caliber. We were flattered by his kind words and did our best to suppress our laughter as he walked away. The inside joke was that only seconds earlier I held up

257

Values

the paper and told my wife the President's daughters reminded me of our two girls.

I read the newspaper article and was filled with pride by the positive adjectives used to describe the Obama family. They are not the stereotypical African American family commonly portrayed on television. I thought, *"What an honor it is to have someone look at <u>MY</u> family and be reminded of something so positive."*

After I finished reading I sat quietly and took an inventory of my blessings. I had so much more than career and financial success. My family was secure. We were respected and had earned a "good name." I recognized my good fortune and was very appreciative. My emotions were touched in an indescribable way. It's difficult to articulate the joy of having a good wife and healthy children. For years, friends had jokingly referred to my family as the Huxtables, Bill Cosby's sit-com family on his 1980's television show. The Bryant's had just

258

Values

received a promotion. If that image now reflected the Obama's I was honored.

I thought, *"How did I get blessed with a family that emanates such a positive impression. Do we inspire people to think optimistically about marriage, parenthood or family values? How could we use it to inspire people to get married, love each other and love their children?"*

Wouldn't it be cool if the next 'thing' became looking and acting 'Presidential'? Can't you see it, young people throughout the country dressing neatly, pulling up their pants, tucking in their shirts and speaking properly? In my opinion, it would be a welcome contrast to the popular fad of tattoos, piercing, cornrows and Afros.

I'm not on the holier than thou high horse and don't mean to impose my values; I just feel blessed to be in a comfortable place and I wish at the very least, everyone experience this level of contentment. I'm

259

Values

---

fully aware that I don't have a monopoly on happiness. What I do have is joy in my heart, purpose in my steps and passion for what I do. For that, I am very thankful because it is much more than I deserve. There are three parts of my life I value deeply and I'm not ashamed to discuss, my family, my community and my faith. They keep me grounded and are the foundation of the vision for my purpose.

Let me start with the family. My wife, Robin, is classy, brilliant and drop-dead gorgeous. She received her bachelor's degree in computer science from Spelman College in Atlanta and her law degree from Creighton University in Omaha. The frick to my frack and the ying to my yang, my soul mate is a strong-minded, opinionated, third generation college graduate as well as third generation AKA (Alpha Kappa Alpha Sorority). She holds a management position with a Fortune 500 company and she manages an interior design partnership in her spare time. Robin is a Christian woman who has no problem with me being the head of the household, because she knows how to keep a brotha' in check. God gave me exactly what I needed...

We have three fantastic children, two girls and one boy. My parenting emphasis mainly focuses on three areas, belief in God, academic excellence and good character. I'm proud to say my children listen and as my mother says, *"They know how to act."* This is an age in which many young people have little and in some cases no respect for their elders. As parents, my wife and I demand respect, but it's not a struggle with our children. They want to please us; we are blessed to have good children.

Our two beautiful daughters are proof the apple didn't fall far from their mother's tree. Our oldest daughter, Brazier, is all girl; sugar and spice and all that's nice. She has a rich brown complexion like her daddy, wavy black hair and is growing into a beautiful young lady. At 16 years old she now

Values

spends more time in the mirror than talking to her dad, but as I understand it, that's par for the course with teenagers. She is a varsity cheerleader, a member of the National Honor Society and is a Master Sergeant in the 99th Pursuit Civil Air Patrol Squadron. She is reserved, quiet and at times introverted but will take the bull by the horns if necessary. Her personality affirms the old saying, "Still waters run deep."

Our second daughter, Madison, was a surprise entry into the family. She is an extremely assertive spirit who does not take a back seat to anyone, especially her older siblings. Madison is competitive, smart and she loves to win. She is an aggressive soccer player who takes piano and dance lessons. Madison has a high amount of compassion and empathy. She displays genuine and sincere concern for people's feelings. Whenever she sees the starving kids in the "Feed the Children" commercials she makes sure we send a donation. At 8 years old she has provided more excitement to our family than we

Values

knew possible. She is a daddy's girl so I'm not ashamed to say she has the looks and charm to be Miss Universe.

Now, the proverbial chip off the old block is my son, Paul Edward Bryant II, a.k.a. PJ. He is my running buddy, my pride and joy. At age 12 he does it all -- computers, reading, basketball and golf. He is an exceptionally bright young man; he represented his school in the city Spelling Bee, participated in the Geography Bee and earned a speaking role in the middle school play; a notable accomplishment for a sixth grader. PJ wears a perpetual smile and easily makes friends. I can't thank God enough for giving me a son; he knew we needed more testosterone in the home. My son has a zest for life, when I look at him it's like looking in the mirror and seeing only the good. What ever it is, that thing we men share about having sons; P.J. gives it to me in abundance. He provides me with many moments to smile inside and say to myself, *"That's my boy!"*

Values

Yes, I'm high on the Bryant family; I'm their biggest fan. They are the flesh of my flesh and the bone of my bone. Shouldn't I be the first person to see their greatness and speak purpose into their lives? I refuse to sit back, wait, or gamble on the chance someone else will. I believe society would have fewer problems if more men put their families on a platform and dedicated themselves to keeping them there. If more daughters heard, *"I love you and your beautiful"* at home, they would be less inclined to fall for those lines in the streets.

Before I boost my parenting skills up too high, let me come clean and admit that I didn't always recognize what a good thing I had. There were times when I didn't appreciate or understand the importance of family life. In my younger days I was ego driven and self-serving. My priorities were making money and gaining recognition. I stepped on, over, and around many people on my race to achieve; including my family. I took everything in

Values

stride like the world owed me something. My family existed strictly for my amusement.

I really can't say what caused the change; maybe it's the wisdom that comes with age; maybe it's recognizing my mortality. The thought of looking back over my life and seeing material success and family failure is haunting. Accepting this revelation while everyone is healthy and times are good is truly a blessing. Now, I am the entertainment. I try my best to make my family members smile each and every day. Sometimes my efforts aggravate them, but no amount of money, career success, or fame comes with more love than my attempts at humor.

I know the truth; the most meaningful and significant elements in my life sleep under my roof. I realize their stay in my house is limited. Many a night I look into their bedrooms while they are sleeping and send up prayers of thanks. If the world operated on a system of universal justice in which

Values

you only received what you deserved, those beds would be empty. The older I get the more I appreciate my family.

When I was young the picture of my future was not this tranquil and serene. My story begins with a modest upbringing in Omaha, Nebraska, the state's largest city with a population of 700,000 in the metropolitan area. The state boasts of being the "Heartland of America." But closer to home is North Omaha, with 60,000 African Americans. It is the Enterprise Zone, the Empowerment Zone, the low-income blighted area, as described on city applications for federal funds. North Omaha has some of the oldest housing in the city and in many areas there are more vacant lots than houses. You can easily find a barbershop or liquor store, but it would be easier to find a needle in a haystack than to find a grocery store, pharmacy or medical office.

North Omaha is the section of the city that officially qualifies as the ghetto. It's the part of town many

Values

well-to-do citizens are afraid to enter. I have to admit, it's no Mayberry. It's the wrong side of the tracks we affectionately call, "the hood." I was raised in a neighborhood four blocks from the 1968 riot. Nobody I grew up with lived a "Leave it to Beaver" life.

When I was growing up everyday was an adventure in the 'hood. We never knew what a new day would bring. At an early age, I had seen it all. Police chases, shootings; stabbings, beat downs, dog fights, spouse fights, shoplifting and drug deals. Innocence and naiveté didn't last long in the ghetto. You had to be on your toes or an unpleasant situation could just walk up and find you. I didn't think we lived in a bad environment. It's all I knew. I didn't have anxiety or fear and I never felt vulnerable. It's a fact, the neighborhood you live in, the school you attend, and your family and friends all have a profound impact on your personality. Growing up in those surroundings gave

267

Values

---

me a sixth sense. I developed the ability to read people and circumstances with quickness.

Even though the majority of residents in "the hood" are hard-working, tax paying, law-abiding citizens who want decent housing, clean neighborhoods and a safe environment to raise children, their photos seldom make the front page of the newspaper.

The origin of North Omaha's negative image dates back to the riots in the 1960s. Like most urban cities during that time, civil unrest hit Omaha. In 1966 a white policeman shot and killed a 14-year-old black girl and the community erupted with burning and looting. The aftermath left desolation and the erosion of the community's business district. The negative perception was further enhanced by the drug wars of the 1980s and '90s. Drive-by shootings from rival street gangs ensured the community received its share of negative press.

Values

Over the past 40 years many attempts at urban renewal have failed and many residents blame the decay on the hesitancy of those with the resources to reinvest in the area. They may have a point. However, I believe that true revival will only come when the people who live in North Omaha stand up, take pride in their surroundings and build from within.

It's extremely important to put your money where your mouth is. I personally rehabilitated five houses and built a home in North Omaha. Even though my family can afford to live in a different sector of the city, North Omaha is our home, it's where I was born, raised and currently prefer to reside.

My father was a custodian, my mother didn't graduate from high school and I was the first person in my family to graduate from college. Gaining an education opened doors I didn't know existed. I'm

Values

living proof it's possible to overcome obstacles and be successful.

One of the lessons I learned was the battle is never over until you decide to quit. You always have a chance if you don't give up. I've taken some of life's toughest body punches and I'm still standing. Some of my former buddies are in prison, strung out on drugs and have been killed. It's a mystery how two people can grow up in the same neighborhood, attend the same schools and one goes to law school and the other goes to prison. I don't know why God blessed me to travel the road I'm on, but I'm ever so thankful He did.

In my opinion, a major reason for many of the problems in inner cities throughout America is the scenario of success for most black people. I have labeled it, the "three get" syndrome:

1. Get a good education...
2. Get a good job...

Values

---

3. Get as far away from the community as
    your salary will allow you to go...

The problem with the "three get" syndrome is it will
make you forget. When the best educated and the
highest paid residents of a community leave, they
are missed. People don't realize their quest for
advancement weakens the community.

And unfortunately, many of them become
carpetbaggers. Behind the pretext of love for the
community, they use their old connections to
maneuver through the neighborhood to do business.
They talk a good game, but in reality they are only
looking to make a buck. Their talk of reinvestment
and economic development is only a smoke screen
to hide their self-interest. For many of these people
their self-worth is measured by their net worth.

I know this firsthand because I was one of them. I
held a six-figure, high visibility, high travel position
that to me was the epitome of career success. I'll

271

Values

admit it; the seductive nature of living in the fast lane caused me to loose track of reality. Few things are more captivating than money, prestige and influence. The airports, hotels, influential and powerful clients almost caused me to overlook the blessings right under my nose, my family and my community. As strange as this seems, the more my job required me to be away from the community, the more opportunities, (boards, commissions, etc.) I was given to lead in the community. My opinions were sought on issues I was not connected with or passionate about. I currently serve as the Executive Director of a non-profit organization located in the heart of the 'hood' and those who seek solutions for the ills of North Omaha no longer seek after my opinions.

I am an opinionated person. There is one thing I am absolutely sure about; there is a God and even though my actions are not always consistent with my beliefs, I know he is real. God has carried me up many a mountain and has led me through

Values

countless valleys. For some reason he has blessed me to live an extremely eventful life. Throughout this book I discuss events, experiences and chance encounters that are absolutely amazing to me. I am constantly asking myself, *"How in the world did you get here?"* In most of these occasions I am in awe of the fact that God has even blessed me to be in the room.

If I look to find the source of my unwavering belief in God; my search for spiritual truth travels a diverse and winding path. When I was a child my brother and I attended Mount Calvary Community church with our mother. On the Sundays she didn't go to church, we went to Sunday school at Clair Methodist Church. At age 15, I branched out on my own and joined Salem Baptist Church, and at age 20 I joined Sharon Seventh-Day-Adventist Church. I stopped attending church completely around the age of 25 and seven years later was married in a Catholic Church at age 32. My wife and I joined Grace Apostolic Church a year after we were

Values

married, and for the past eight years my family's membership has been with the Salem Baptist Church.

I think it is unusual for someone to have such a diverse list of spiritual memberships; maybe not... I believe I've grown from having different denominational experiences and feel my appreciation for different faiths give me a unique perspective of God. To my family's dismay, I am the guy who invites the Jehovah's Witnesses and the Mormon missionaries inside to talk...

I have an extremely optimistic outlook on life; the glass of water is definitely half-full. I look for, anticipate and expect good things to happen. A person's attitude determines their altitude. People who possess lowly graveyard dispositions end up in situations worthy of their personality. It's a self-fulfilling prophecy. The world will render you exactly what you expect. We are the sum total of our thoughts.

Values

God has blessed me with the ability to withstand the disappointments of life's cellar and he has given me the opportunity to appreciate the view from the penthouse. I've always felt there was a purpose for my life. As far back as I can remember unusual events have happened to me. The following two incidents happened when I was a child; they led me to believe I had a guardian angel protecting me.

When I was 4 years old, my mother took me to the hospital, I had been sick for several days and unfortunately; the home remedy of rest and chicken noodle soup didn't work. My mother was standing at the admissions counter filling out forms when I lost consciousness, fell to the floor and produced a puddle of green vomit in the lobby.

I was unconscious, so the rest of this story is my mother's version of what happened next. It's an account I've heard her tell many times. A janitor appeared out of nowhere. He scooped me up in one arm and started running down the hallway. He

Values

opened a door and ran down a stairwell. My mother looked at the woman behind the counter, who looked back at her and shrugged her shoulders. My mother left everything at the counter and ran as fast as she could to catch up with the mysterious janitor. She ran down the stairwell and come out in the Emergency Room. She saw the janitor run past the admittance counter to the first doctor he could find. The doctor took one look at the vomit and bellowed to the staff, *"Get prepped for operation. His appendix just burst."* They operated right there on the spot! After the procedure the doctor told my mother, *"Five minutes later, and he would have died."*

I have a seven-inch scar on my stomach as a reminder of that close encounter with death. My mother says the janitor disappeared as mysteriously as he emerged. He didn't give his name and no one on staff seemed to know who he was.

Values

I owe my life to an unknown janitor. This is one reason I give eye contact and speak to people regardless of their title or position. It's important to show everyone respect; every janitor, waiter or homeless person on the street. You never know, you could be speaking to an angel.

Another life threatening incident happened to me when I was 8 years old. I ran into the street without looking and was hit by a car. Everything about this event was totally my fault. For starters, I was not supposed to be crossing the street. I was trying to cross the street as quickly as possible so I wouldn't get caught. I looked back toward my house to make sure no one was looking, and then darted between two parked cars into the street. The driver of the approaching vehicle didn't see me or have time to apply his brakes. I stepped in front of his car and the next thing I knew I was flying. The sky and the ground rotated in slow motion as I flipped through the air. I landed on the curb and instantly jumped to

Values

---

my feet. Everything occurred so fast I really didn't know what happened.

Thank God, it's a miracle I wasn't hurt. I was most terrified by the immediate attention, it seemed that everyone in the neighborhood was sitting on their front porch. They all rushed from their houses toward me. The driver of the car grabbed my arm. *"Are you all right? Are you OK?"* The look in his eye and his grip on my arm let me know he was as angry as he was afraid. As soon as he let my arm go, I bolted across the street and headed home, zigzagging through the neighborhood so he couldn't follow me. I learned first hand the importance of looking both ways before crossing the street.

I ran directly in front of moving car and took a frontal hit. The driver didn't have time to apply his brakes or change directions. Why did I fly through the air instead of roll under his bumper? That unknown janitor at the hospital could have done nothing or simply called for a doctor instead of

278

---

taking immediate action; why? Some people will look at these outcomes and say they were either luck or good fortune. What do I think? At a young and impressionable age I survived two life-threatening experiences. My Grandmother told me I had a guardian angel protecting me; making sure I fulfilled my purpose. I believe her.

This childhood conviction allowed me to hold my head high in the face of adversity. It provided the inner strength to persevere when the odds were stacked heavily against me. I always felt top-shelf even when circumstances said I was bargain basement. When I'm passionate for a cause, I will stand alone if necessary.

My children tell me I have a propensity lecture. I've been told I can be 'preachy' when I want to prove a point. I try my best to be considerate. If my enthusiasm seems zealous, it's only because time is short, the clock is ticking and it's hard to sit quietly when you have purpose.

Values

One of my major pet peeves is men who don't recognize the anointing of being a father. They dismiss the responsibilities of leadership and willingly relinquish their title of father to be called a "Baby's Daddy." The term implies that the man was only involved in the conception of the child. Much too often, it's the mother who shoulders the responsibility of both raising the children and financially supporting the family. Is it any surprise the crown of father has been replaced with Baby's Daddy?

We must acknowledge spiritual warfare; there is an effort to destroy the relationship between fathers and their children; to obliterate the family. Cut off the head and the body will follow. Many young people do not view their fathers as servant leaders. They see them as takers who never contribute; Predators that come around to take food, money, love or simply mom's attention. If the father loses his place of dignity and respect in the family his children are headed down an uncertain path.

Values

Children will have a hard time respecting the celestial father if they have no respect for their earthly father. A child whose only experience is with a Baby's Daddy will find it difficult to understand the love and loyalty of the heavenly father. Why is this important? Someone with no positive connection to their past, who lacks pride, will discover little to value. And people, who find little value on their own life, will find little to value in yours. Society will suffer if the number of Baby Daddies continues to multiply.

When I was in college, success was having a six-figure salary and a Vice President title. Now Ralph Waldo Emerson's poem, Success, has deeper meaning.

Success is to laugh often and much, to earn the affection of small children and the appreciation of honest critics. To endure the betrayal of false friends, to always see the best in others, to appreciate beauty, to make the world a better place

281

Values

whether by a healthy child, a redeemed social condition, or just a garden patch. To know that one life has breathed a little easier is to have succeeded.

What do you value? What are the issues in life you hold strong opinions about? Find those things and hold on to them; never let them go because therein lie the keys to happiness. What a tragedy it would be to just exist; to live out everyday without having something to be passionate for.

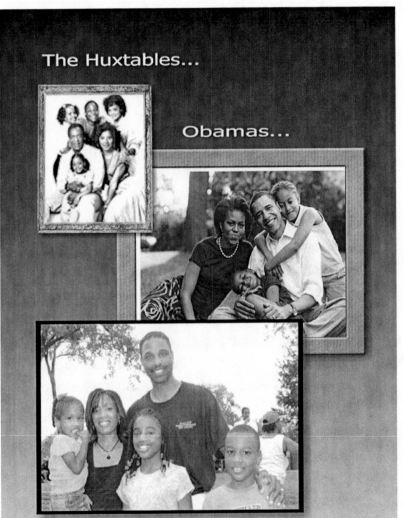

The Huxtables...

Obamas...

and the Bryants...

Chapter Fourteen

Legacy

Have you said anything worth remembering?

A Purpose Living Leader will leave a Legacy. What will people remember about you? When the final curtain is called on the performance of your life, which of your deeds will the audience commit to memory? There are several Leaders who stand out in my mind; their legacies will impact people for generations. They are my Purpose Living, Legacy Leaving, Leader Hall of Fame. This list consists of Dr. Martin Luther King Jr., John F. Kennedy, Nelson Mandela, Mother Teresa, Mohatma Ghandi, Barack Obama and Jesus Christ.

I read these quotes as a source of inspiration and encouragement. The insight and depth of their words will be forever etched in the archives of

284

Legacy

humanity. The following quotations are my favorites. It's not what you say; it's what you do that's important. Read their words and judge for yourself, did they walk the talk or just, talk the talk?

Dr. Martin Luther King Jr.

A genuine leader is not a searcher for consensus but a molder of consensus...

A nation that continues year after year to spend more money on military defense than on programs of social uplift is approaching spiritual doom...

An individual has not started living until he can rise above the narrow confines of his individualistic concerns to the broader concerns of all humanity....

Change does not roll in on the wheels of inevitability, but comes through continuous struggle. And so we must straighten our backs and

Legacy

work for our freedom. A man can't ride you unless your back is bent....

Every man must decide whether he will walk in the light of creative altruism or in the darkness of destructive selfishness...

Faith is taking the first step even when you don't see the whole staircase...

History will have to record that the greatest tragedy of this period of social transition was not the strident clamor of the bad people, but the appalling silence of the good people...

I have a dream that my four little children will one day live in a nation where they will not be judged by the color of their skin, but by the content of their character...

I refuse to accept the view that mankind is so tragically bound to the starless midnight of racism

Legacy

and war that the bright daybreak of peace and brotherhood can never become a reality...

I believe that unarmed truth and unconditional love will have the final word...

If physical death is the price that I must pay to free my white brothers and sisters from a permanent death of the spirit, then nothing can be more redemptive...

Injustice anywhere is a threat to justice everywhere...

Life's most persistent and urgent question is, 'What are you doing for others?'...

Love is the only force capable of transforming an enemy into friend...

Legacy

The means we use must be as pure as the ends we seek. Never forget that everything Hitler did in Germany was legal...

One who breaks an unjust law that conscience tells him is unjust, and who willingly accepts the penalty of imprisonment in order to arouse the conscience of the community over its injustice, is in reality expressing the highest respect for law....

Our scientific power has outrun our spiritual power. We have guided missiles and misguided men...

Philanthropy is commendable, but it must not cause the philanthropist to overlook the circumstances of economic injustice, which make philanthropy necessary...

Rarely do we find men who willingly engage in hard, solid thinking. There is an almost universal quest for easy answers and half-baked solutions.

Legacy

Nothing pains some people more than having to think...

The function of education is to teach one to think intensively and to think critically. Intelligence plus character – that is the goal of true education...

The hottest place in Hell is reserved for those who remain neutral in times of great moral conflict...

The moral arc of the universe bends at the elbow of justice...

The ultimate measure of a man is not where he stands in moments of comfort and convenience, but where he stands at times of challenge and controversy...

War is a poor chisel to carve out tomorrow...

We must build dikes of courage to hold back the flood of fear...

Legacy

We must use time creatively...

Whatever affects one directly, affects all indirectly. I can never be what I ought to be until you are what you ought to be. This is the interrelated structure of reality...

John F. Kennedy

A nation, which has forgotten the quality of courage, which in the past has been brought to public life, is not as likely to insist upon or regard that quality in its chosen leaders – and in fact, we have forgotten...

Efforts and courage are not enough without purpose and direction....

I look forward to a great future for America – a future in which our country will match its military

Legacy

strength with our moral restraint, its wealth with our wisdom, its power with our purpose...

Leadership and learning are indispensable to each other....

Our progress as a nation can be no swifter than our progress in education. The human mind is our fundamental resource....

The courage of life is often a less dramatic spectacle than the courage of a final moment; but it is no less a magnificent mixture of triumph and tragedy...

Skeptics or cynics whose horizons are limited by the obvious realities cannot possibly solve the problems of the world. We need men who can dream of things that never were...

We have the power to make this the best generation of mankind in the history of the world or to make it the last...

Legacy

We must use time as a tool, not as a couch...

Nelson Mandela

After climbing a great hill, one only finds that there are many more hills to climb...

Education is the most powerful weapon, which you can use to change the world...

I learned that courage was not the absence of fear, but the triumph over it. The brave man is not he who does not feel afraid, but he who conquers that fear...

If you talk to a man in a language he understands, that goes to his head. If you talk to him in his language, that goes to his heart...

In my country we go to prison first and then become President....

Legacy

It is better to lead from behind and to put others in front, especially when you celebrate victory. You take the front line when there is danger. Then people will appreciate your leadership....

Money won't create success, the freedom to make it will...

The greatest glory in living lies not in never falling, but in rising every time we fall....

There is no passion to be found playing small – in settling for a life that is less than the one you are capable of living...

We must use time wisely and forever realize that the time is always ripe to do right...

Mother Teresa

Be faithful in small things because it is in them that your strength lays...

293

Legacy

Do not wait for leaders; do it alone, person to person...

Even the rich are hungry for love, for being cared for, for being wanted, for having someone to call their own...

I do not pray for success, I ask for faithfulness...

I know God will not give me anything I can't handle. I just wish that He didn't trust me so much....

I want you to be concerned about your next-door neighbor. Do you know your next-door neighbor?

If we have no peace, it is because we have forgotten that we belong to each other...

If you can't feed a hundred people, then feed just one...

294

Legacy

It is poverty to decide that a child must die so that you may live as you wish...

It is not the magnitude of our actions but the amount of love that is put into them that matters....

Let us always meet each other with smile, for the smile is the beginning of love....

Let us touch the dying, the poor, the lonely and the unwanted according to the graces we have received and let us not be ashamed or slow to do the humble work...

One of the greatest diseases is to be nobody to anybody....

Spread love everywhere you go. Let no one ever come to you without leaving happier...

Legacy

There must be a reason why some people can afford to live well. They must have worked for it. I only feel angry when I see waste.

We can do no great things, only small things with great love....

We ourselves feel that what we are doing is just a drop in the ocean. But the ocean would be less because of that missing drop...

We, the unwilling, led by the unknowing, are doing the impossible for the ungrateful. We have done so much, for so long, with so little, we are now qualified to do anything with nothing....

Mahatma Ghandi

A 'No' uttered from the deepest conviction is better than a 'Yes' merely uttered to please, or worse, to avoid trouble....

Legacy

A man is but the product of his thoughts what he thinks, he becomes...

A nation's culture resides in the hearts and in the soul of its people...

A small body of determined spirits fired by an unquenchable faith in their mission can alter the course of history...

All the religions of the world, while they may differ in other respects, united proclaim that nothing lives in this world but Truth...

Always aim at complete harmony of thought and word and deed. Always aim at purifying your thoughts and everything will be well...

Be the change that you want to see in the world...

Even if you are a minority of one, the truth is the truth...

297

Legacy

Fear has its use but cowardice has none...

First they ignore you, then they laugh at you, then they fight you, then you win...

Happiness is when what you think, what you say, and what you do are in harmony...

I suppose leadership at one time meant muscles; but today it means getting along with people....

If patience is worth anything, it must endure to the end of time. And a living faith will last in the midst of the blackest storm...

Imitation is the sincerest flattery...

It is the quality of our work, which will please God and not the quantity...

Live as if you were to die tomorrow. Learn as if you were to live forever...

Legacy

My life is my message…

No culture can live if it attempts to be exclusive…

Nobody can hurt me without my permission…

Power is of two kinds. One is obtained by the fear of punishment and the other by acts of love. Power based on love is a thousand times more effective and permanent then the one derived from fear of punishment…

The best way to find yourself is to lose yourself in the service of others…

The moment there is suspicion about a person's motives, everything he does becomes tainted…

There are people in the world so hungry, that God cannot appear to them except in the form of bread…

Legacy

There is nothing that wastes the body like worry, and one who has any faith in God should be ashamed to worry about anything whatsoever...

Those who say religion has nothing to do with politics do not know what religion is....

Unwearied ceaseless effort is the price that must be paid for turning faith into a rich infallible experience...

What difference does it make to the dead, the orphans, and the homeless, whether the mad destruction is wrought under the name of totalitarianism or the holy name of liberty or democracy?

You can chain me, you can torture me, you can even destroy this body, but you will never imprison my mind...

300

Legacy

You don't have to burn books to destroy a culture. Just get people to stop reading them...

Barack Obama

Change will not come if we wait for some other person or some other time. We are the ones we've been waiting for. We are the change that we seek... Focusing your life solely on making a buck shows a certain poverty of ambition. It asks too little of yourself. Because it's only when you hitch your wagon to something larger than yourself that you realize your true potential...

I think when you spread the wealth around it's good for everybody...

If you're walking down the right path and you're willing to keep walking, eventually you'll make progress...

Legacy

Today we begin in earnest the work of making sure that the world we leave our children is just a little bit better than the one we inhabit today...

The fact that my 15 minutes of fame has extended a little longer than 15 minutes is somewhat surprising to me and completely baffling to my wife...

There are patriots who opposed the war in Iraq and there are patriots who supported the war in Iraq. We are one people, all of us pledging allegiance to the stars and stripes, all of us defending the United States of America...

There is not a liberal America and a conservative America – there is the United States of America. There is not a black America and a white America and Latino America and Asian America – there's the United States of America...

This is the moment when we must come together to save this planet. Let us resolve that we will not

Legacy

leave our children a world where the oceans rise and famine spreads and terrible storms devastate our lands...

We can't drive our SUVs and eat as much as we want and keep our homes on 72 degrees at all times and then just expect that other countries are going to say OK. That's not leadership...

We have an obligation and a responsibility to be investing in our students and our schools. We must make sure that people, who have the grades, the desire and the will, but not the money, can still get the best education possible...

We need to internalize this idea of excellence. Not many folks spend a lot of time trying to be excellent...

We need to steer clear of this poverty of ambition, where people want to drive fancy cars and wear nice clothes and live in nice apartments but don't

Legacy

want to work hard to accomplish these things. Everyone should try to realize his or her full potential...

Jesus Christ

Blessed are the poor in spirit, for theirs is the kingdom of heaven...

Blessed are those who mourn, for they will be comforted...

Blessed are the meek, for they will inherit the earth...

Blessed are those who hunger and thirst for righteousness, for they will be filled...

Blessed are the merciful, for they will be shown mercy...

Legacy

Blessed are the pure in heart, for they will see God...

Blessed are the peacemakers, for they will be called sons of God...

Blessed are those who are persecuted because of righteousness, for theirs is the kingdom of heaven...

Blessed are you when people insult you, persecute you and falsely say all kinds of evil against you because of me...

Rejoice and be glad, because great is your reward in heaven, for in the same way they persecuted the prophets who were before you...

Salt and Light

You are the salt of the earth. But if the salt loses its saltiness, how can it be made salty again? It is no longer good for anything, except to be thrown out and trampled by men...

305

Legacy

You are the light of the world. A city on a hill cannot be hidden...

Neither do people light a lamp and put it under a bowl. Instead they put it on its stand, and it gives light to everyone in the house...

In the same way, let your light shine before men, that they may see your good deeds and praise your Father in heaven...

The Fulfillment of the Law

Do not think that I have come to abolish the Law or the Prophets; I have not come to abolish them but to fulfill them...

I tell you the truth, until heaven and earth disappear, not the smallest letter, not the least stroke of a pen, will by any means disappear from the Law until everything is accomplished...

Legacy

Anyone who breaks one of the least of these commandments and teaches others to do the same will be called least in the kingdom of heaven, but whoever practices and teaches these commands will be called great in the kingdom of heaven...

For I tell you that unless your righteousness surpasses that of the Pharisees and the teachers of the law, you will certainly not enter the kingdom of heaven.

Murder

You have heard that it was said to the people long ago, Do not murder, and anyone who murders will be subject to judgment...

But I tell you that anyone who is angry with his brother will be subject to judgment. Again, anyone who says to his brother, 'Raca, is answerable to the Sanhedrin. But anyone who says, 'You fool!' will be in danger of the fire of hell...

Legacy

Therefore, if you are offering your gift at the altar and there remember that your brother has something against you; leave your gift there in front of the altar. First go and be reconciled to your brother; then come and offer your gift...

Settle matters quickly with your adversary who is taking you to court. Do it while you are still with him on the way, or he may hand you over to the judge, and the judge may hand you over to the officer, and you may be thrown into prison...

I tell you the truth, you will not get out until you have paid the last penny.

Adultery

You have heard that it was said, Do not commit adultery...

But I tell you that anyone who looks at a woman lustfully has already committed adultery with her in his heart...

Legacy

If your right eye causes you to sin, gouge it out and throw it away. It is better for you to lose one part of your body than for your whole body to be thrown into hell...

And if your right hand causes you to sin, cut it off and throw it away. It is better for you to lose one part of your body than for your whole body to go into hell...

Divorce

It has been said, Anyone who divorces his wife must give her a certificate of divorce...

But I tell you that anyone who divorces his wife, except for marital unfaithfulness, causes her to become an adulteress, and anyone who marries the divorced woman commits adultery.

Legacy

Oaths

Again, you have heard that it was said to the people long ago, Do not break your oath, but keep the oaths you have made to the Lord...

But I tell you, Do not swear at all: either by heaven, for it is God's throne; or by the earth, for it is his footstool; or by Jerusalem, for it is the city of the Great King...

And do not swear by your head, for you cannot make even one hair white or black...

Simply let your 'Yes' be 'Yes,' and your 'No,' 'No'; anything beyond this comes from the evil one...

An Eye for an Eye

You have heard that it was said, 'Eye for eye, and tooth for tooth...

Legacy

But I tell you, Do not resist an evil person. If someone strikes you on the right cheek, turn to him the other also...

And if someone wants to sue you and take your tunic, let him have your cloak as well. [41]If someone forces you to go one mile, go with him two miles...

Give to the one who asks you, and do not turn away from the one who wants to borrow from you.

Love for Enemies
You have heard that it was said, Love your neighbor and hate your enemy...

But I tell you: Love your enemies and pray for those who persecute you, that you may be sons of your Father in heaven. He causes his sun to rise on the evil and the good, and sends rain on the righteous and the unrighteous...

Legacy

If you love those who love you, what reward will you get? Are not even the tax collectors doing that?

And if you greet only your brothers, what are you doing more than others? Do not even pagans do that?

Be perfect, therefore, as your heavenly Father is perfect.

> *"If you hold to my teaching, you are really my disciples. Then you will know the truth, and the truth will set you free."*
>
> *- Jesus Christ*

Purpose Living Leaders challenge us to reach for a higher standard. The members of my Purpose Living Leaders Hall of Fame are worthy of our respect and adulation because they stood for something. They encouraged us to reach deep within ourselves to find greatness. They overcame

Legacy

---

obstacles, reached the pinnacle of success and inspired us to do, be, and become more. They were more concerned with fulfilling their purpose than filling their pockets. These altruistic Legacy-Leaving Leaders stood out, because they stood up.

Chapter Fifteen

Validation

What are others saying about you?

So, you think you have purpose. Does your career determine your purpose? Is it your passions, your community involvement? How do you know if you are fulfilling it? Is there any concrete evidence that affirms someone is doing what they were placed on this earth to do?

I know this, when someone is in his or her zone its evident and obvious to everyone around them. They have an aura of intention. One way to tell is by what observers say about them; people who have no vested interest in the outcome of their efforts.

I have felt like I was in the zone for the past four years. Nurturing and developing future leaders feels right for me, it fits like a comfortable pair of

Validation

hush puppies. The following articles are what others have said about my involvement with the Wesley House Leadership Academy.

Non Profit Back in Business

New Director Starts To Ease Historic Agency Out Of Troubled Times
By ERIN GRACE, *STAFF WRITER*
Reprint from Omaha WORLD-HERALD
Tuesday, July 19, 2005

Nine boys in summer clothes slid their arms into crisp navy blue blazers. They fingered the buttons, played with the lapels and giggled self-consciously moments before their Monday morning entrance into a room of ministers and the news media. *"You guys look sharp,"* Paul Bryant, new director of the Wesley House, told them. *"I'm very proud of you."* The boys, participating in a summer academy at north Omaha's Wesley House, weren't the only ones making an entrance.

315

Validation

Bryant, a former Gallup executive whose jobs in recent years have included small-business owner, Urban League interim director and Wells Fargo banker, also announced his new role. As executive director of the United Methodist Community Centers Inc.-Wesley House, his job is to get the historic nonprofit agency back on its feet.

Since 2003, the organization has lost its United Way funding and affiliation, its job helping troubled youths in the court system, its director and its staff. When Bryant was hired May 16, he said the agency was $40,000 in debt. But Bryant said he was attracted to the challenge, the potential and to helping revive the 133-year-old agency.

He said he has met two initial goals – raising $40,000 to cancel the debt and starting a summer academy for boys' ages 7 to 10, Bryant said he is focusing on black youths because they most need the support. He wants to reach children before they make poor choices – to nurture interests in books,

Validation

speech and debate, chess and other activities that stir the brain. *"We're focusing on trying to create a place where young people can just be challenged and learn,"* said Dan Johnston, president of the Wesley House board.

But the children in class Monday didn't seem to mind showing off their firm handshakes. Wesley House charges $50 a week for five full days of structured activities. Boys get breakfast and lunch, exercise class, field trips and training to strengthen writing, public speaking, decision-making, character and etiquette. Uniforms, including the navy jackets, will be worn on special occasions. A few youngsters have left since the program started in June. Some nodded when asked whether it seemed like they were still in school. But all agreed they loved the field trips and a chance to spend the day with friends. *"We're trying to make learning fun,"* explained 9-year-old Khalil Grant. *"We're doing a lot of other fun stuff."*

317

Validation

Bridging the Gap
Paul Bryant leads Wesley House's Rebirth
by Leo Adam Biga
Reprint from The Reader: June 15 –21 2006

Thirteen months ago Paul Bryant left behind a fat banking career to lead the Wesley House, 2001 N. 35th Street, a once proud United Methodist Community Center beset by problems. Under his aegis the agency's gained a new lease on life as the Wesley House Leadership Academy of Academic and Artistic Excellence.

As executive director Bryant's embarking on year two of a program to nurture high achievement among inner city children through tutoring, academic and life skills training and enrichment activities. Students are taught everything from small business and stock market concepts to good manners. Kids greet visitors with a firm handshake, direct eye contact and the words "Welcome to the Wesley House." An ACADEMIC Summer Academy targets boys ages 7-12. An after-school

Validation

program works with boys and girls, ages 7-12, over the school year.

In the Wesley's brick and glass building the hope stirred by the new program is expressed in the eager faces, urgent voices and insistent raised hands of children vying for coveted blue blazers. The jackets are reserved for students who demonstrate a grasp of business principles usually taught in high school or college.

In the spare conference room where he teaches a Business in the Boardroom class to 3rd and 4th graders, Bryant fits the exec profile with his crisp attire, tall frame and on-point demeanor. Sounding variously like a banker, brother, father, teacher and preacher, he aims to build broad- based support wherever he can, Bryant puts the boys, many from single-parent homes, through their paces. Most are too small to rest their elbows on the table. *"What's the calculation for a balance sheet?"* In unison, they answer, *"Assets minus liabilities equals net*

319

Validation

*worth." "What about an income statement?"
"Revenues minus expenses equals net income."
"When an asset loses value, what's that called?"
"Depreciation." "What is it when it gains value?"
"Appreciation."*

What may seem too dry or advanced is fun. *"It's structured, it's cerebral, and they like **it**. They're not bouncing off the walls,"* he said. *"This is a 'Please' and 'Thank you,' 'Yes, ma'am' and 'No, sir' environment. There's no sagging here. You've got to pull your pants up. There's no cursing, no fighting. You can lose your privileges. That's just the way it is, and we're not apologetic about it."* Holding kids to a higher plane is what it's all about. Bryant feels so strongly about it that his son, Paul, attends the academy after-school program.

"We're changing lives," Bryant said. *"I truly believe that. There's a lot of programs that teach our kids how to score baskets and touchdowns and everything else, but we're teaching them how to*

Validation

think and how to operate in the real world." A lifetime Omahan and a member of the storied Bryant-Fisher family that owns a long history of community service here, Bryant volunteered summers in an after-school program operated by Wesley, located near where he grew up. He knew first-hand the positive activities offered there. When he heard about its problems, he felt *"an obligation"* to help rescue what's been a community anchor.

Founded as the Omaha City Mission by the Christian Workers Association in 1872, Wesley is the state's oldest social service agency. Like the underprivileged it serves, the agency has seen hard times, but nothing like the financial quagmire that closed its doors early 2005. *"I said, 'Not the Wesley House. Not another minority-managed organization going down the tubes on hard times. The Wesley House can't go down,"* Bryant recalled. He applied for the vacant top spot and got it, going from corporate banker to head of a troubled non-profit. *"I was a leader looking for an organization and this is*

321

Validation

an organization that's in dire need of some leadership," he said. *"My challenge is to bring this organization to its rightful place of prominence in this community."* Eyebrows arched and tongues wagged when he left a Wells Fargo VP post to start from scratch with a tarnished agency seemingly on its last legs. He's fine going from a sure thing to a long shot – and taking a pay cut – as long as kids succeed.

"My happiness really is not associated with money. Wealth isn't the end all. It's what you do," he said. *"I've had dinner with President Clinton, I've had lunch with Colin Powell. I've had cocktails with Henry Kissinger. I've taken a seven-day cruise with Oprah Winfrey. I've been in Evander Holyfield's house. My biggest client was Isaiah Thomas, I got no better feeling being in any of those circumstances than I do being with these kids here. When I see them get it. When I see them desire those blazers ... I mean, they want 'em. They want 'em bad."*

Validation

Bryant, who holds master's degrees in urban studies and urban education, is not an academic, per Se, but he professes to know what ails the community he calls home. *"I'm from this community. I'm a Bryant-Fisher. I don't need to do scientific research to know what goes on. I see a culture floundering to find relevance in society post-Martin Luther King, Jr. – how to fit into a society that really hasn't found the value in who you are, and still be true to and proud of who you are.* "Somehow, we've got to a point in the inner city where black people think being smart is white behavior, and we've got to change that. This is a community that's not identified by its talent. Ask anybody. Close your eyes and picture a junior high school African-American male. The mental picture you have isn't going to be of a magna cum laude. But there is no correlation between intellect and income at birth. It's a matter of what kids are exposed to. We've got to start identifying the success stories, the kids who like to read and write and learn science."

323

Validation

He said the Gallup Organization surveyed the boys in last year's academy and found some *"have higher expectations than their parents. We want to raise standards, and we work with parents to do that."* He said post-testing revealed an increase in kids' self-esteem. Anecdotally, the students seem to be doing better in school. *"What we want to do is expose inner-city kids to cerebral activities and create an environment where it's cool to be smart,"* he said. *"Our motto is, 'Smart people win.' If you come here and pick up a book, nobody's going to call you egghead and push you around and take your lunch money. If you want to write, we encourage you. We want the smart kids to know they're not islands. We tell them, 'If you stay in school and get good grades, you're going to be at the top of your class and get a scholarship to college. And if you keep getting good grades, you're going to get a good job. If you keep your nose to the grindstone, it's really going to pay off."*

Validation

His message has reached others. At a March 9 press conference he trotted out reps from many partnering organizations. Tutors from UNO, Creighton University, Metro and the Civil Air Patrol aid students with homework and "augment the educational process" with special training in math, reading, the arts, science, technology, etc. Kids display their handiwork in fairs and exhibits. They learn about different careers from professionals they meet on field trips or at Wesley. They track and trade stocks. Their summer garden project is also a small business venture.

A partnership with Mutual of Omaha has created the Technology Project, a pilot program to help bridge the digital divide. Mutual is to donate 60 computers annually to the Wesley House for use by kids in an on-site computer lab now under development and for ACADEMIC Summer Academy students to use at home.

Validation

If he can secure funding, Bryant envisions *"keeping these kids together for 10 years. At that point, they're going to be a group of smart young men that understand public and private sector finance and economics. They can truly help make north Omaha a vital part of the city's growth and development."*

He has plans for early childhood and teen programs. Opening an academy in an area primarily associated with remedial and recreation programs is a bold move for an agency that appeared on its way out. Before its recent makeover, Wesley provided services to youth in the state juvenile justice system. When juvenile justice staff aired concerns over program outcomes and reporting methods, referrals dropped. Soon, United Way raised questions about *"the effectiveness"* of Wesley programs and services. By 2003, all UW money was pulled. Wesley shifted to serving youth and families in the foster care system, but couldn't bring in enough clients. With the loss of officials' trust and a steady revenue stream, it exhausted $500,000 in reserves

Validation

on operating expenses, saw its executive director resign and let go all staff and shut down all programs.

Wesley board chairman Dan Johnston confirmed closing the venerable institution was an option, but a decision was made *"to give it one more good shot."* By then, Wesley was decades removed from its days as a model community revitalization engine in the 1960s-early '70s "War on Poverty." It was the agency's shining hour. Money poured in and national recognition followed initiatives to empower blacks. Then-executive director Rodney Wead led efforts that spawned a black-owned radio station (KOWH), community bank (Community Bank of Nebraska), credit union (Franklin Federal Community Credit Union), minority scholarship program and an ethnic culture center. Later, north side redevelopment organizations led by Michael Maroney (New Community Development Corporation) and Alvin Goodwin (Omaha

327

Validation

Economic Development Corporation) sprung up there.

Although Wesley receives some United Methodist church support, it's long drawn most funding from the United Way and other public/private sources, leaving it vulnerable to the vicissitudes of donors. Only 13 months into Bryant's reign the center is still reeling from the aftermath of the United Way pull out. That severing meant the loss of not only hard-to-replace monies – some $300,000 annually – but the even more valuable endorsement that comes with UW support.

Aware of how much stature Wesley lost in the eyes of the establishment, Bryant, a paradox of by-the-numbers-cruncher, deeply spiritual Christian and community-minded legacy-keeper, approaches his task to reinvent and redeem the agency as nothing less than a calling from above. To justify leaving behind a six- figure income with Wells Fargo (previous to that he was at Gallup and First National

Validation

Bank), he's put aside cold hard calculations. *"I am operating on faith every step of the way,"* he said. *"My moves have not been thought out, studied and projected. When I accepted this job I didn't have any staff. We had no revenues and a $40,000 debt I'd just found out about. I took a leap of faith. Quite frankly, I don't have five-year projections. Right now, it's a matter of survival for this organization. But, hey, I'm on a mission and I'm not too proud to beg."*

Bryant also felt it was time to give back. *"I was at a point in my life when I was really looking for significance, and I felt this is what I'm supposed to do."* The agency's bleak prospects gave him pause, but not enough to deter him. *"I just felt pricked in my heart. Something's got to be done, I thought."* In short order, he introduced his new vision and set about restoring the agency's good name. He promised to retire its $40,000 debt in a Biblically-inspired 40 days. He wiped out the deficit in 36 days. But getting there was never a sure thing. *"I*

Validation

can't tell you how nervous I was," he said. "It wasn't like I had some trump card up my sleeve. The fact is I didn't have some big corporation in my hip pocket. I stepped out on faith and it happened. Just like this new direction we're going. The largest contribution was $5,000. There was only one of those. There were several $1,000 donations. The rest was a whole lot of $500, $100, $25, $10 and $5 checks."

The margin for error is still slim given the $20,000 in monthly operating expenses. *"When I came, we had two weeks before our doors could be shut. Now, we've probably got a two-month cushion. We are not where we need to be but things are looking much better then they were this time last year,"* he said. Another concern is the small number of children being served. Sixteen boys graduated last summer's academy. A Summer Fun Club has 24 kids signed up. About 48 kids attended this past school year's after-school program. It's not all about numbers, but as numbers go, monies flow.

Validation

That's why Bryant hopes to see a spike in enrollees. To bolster the financial footing, ensure continued operations and endow future growth, he counts on grant applications paying off. Getting back in the UW's good graces is another goal. He's also organized benefit events involving Omaha native and pro football Hall of Famer Gale Sayers and his wife, Ardie, who've made Wesley their official Omaha charity. An April 28 screening of *Brian's Song* (the story of Gale Sayers and Brian Piccolo's bond) raised $2,000, enough to pay off a line of credit.

On June 19, the Gale Sayers Wesley House (Golf) Classic is set for the Players Club at Deer Creek. Hitting the links will be National Baseball Hall of Famer Ferguson Jenkins, Heisman Trophy winner Johnny Rodgers, Cornhusker legend Jerry Tagge, the NFL's first black quarterback in Marlin Briscoe, former NBA All-Star Bob Boozer and Creighton University head basketball coach Dana Altman. Tee-off is 10 a.m. Bryant knows public events can only do so much. Bottom line, he must prove the agencies back with a sustainable niche others buy into. One sign he's staying is the new house he and wife Robin built in the nearby Miami Heights development.

"It's about longevity. There are a lot of people who've heard about the bad recent history and they want to see if this is a flash in the pan. Will it still be here? Will I still be here? I can't see going anywhere. I want to be part of the solution. I want to be a bridge-builder." To bridge the achievement gap. The desired end result is summed up in the• academy creed the kids recite from memory. It ends with, *"Through self discipline we will grow into adults of honor and integrity. Our Legacy will be a source of pride to our families and communities."*

Validation

Building on Faith
by Michael Watkins,
Reprint from MetroMagazine
September 2007

Two years ago before leaving his six-figure salary
and vice president position with Wells Fargo, Paul
Bryant would have been sweltering in a blue
pinstriped suit, white collared shirt and coordination
tie and most likely wing-tipped shoes. But these
days as the executive director at the Wesley House
Leadership Academy of Academic and Artistic
Excellence (formerly the Wesley House) on North
35th Street, Bryant is cool and comfortable in blue
jeans, a golf shirt and sandals at the office. And
despite the cut in pay and change in surroundings
coupled with the constant pressure to continue to
lead an organization that deeply and directly
impacts the North Omaha community it serves –
especially the children who come through the
Wesley House doors each day – Bryant has never
been happier or more challenged. He wouldn't

Validation

have it any other way. In many ways, it's his calling.

"Ralph Waldo Emerson said: "Success is to laugh often and much. To earn the affection of small children, and the appreciation of honest critics. To endure the betrayal of false friends, and to always see the best in others. To appreciate beauty. To make the world a little better, whether by a health child, a redeemed social condition, or a garden patch. To know that one life has breathed a little easier because you have lived is to have succeeded." I get to absorb this poem every day in the work that I do and children and families that we impact," Bryant said. *"When a child comes up and hugs me because I made a difference in his or her life, that's worth more than all the money I left behind at the bank. It's priceless, really."*

Priceless but definitely not easy. Having volunteered at the organization as a child, when Bryant first learned of Wesley House's search for

Validation

an executive Director, he was interested but wary of its deep debt and loss of annual funding from the United Way of the Midlands. He was also taken aback by the fact that Wesley House – Omaha's oldest social service agency dating back 135 years in the community – was closed in 2005 due to poor money management. But deep inside, he knew God was calling him to take a chance and bring the organization back into the black – and back to the people who needed its message, guidance and structure most. *"I looked at the numbers one night before going to bed, and it just really looked almost hopeless for Wesley House."* Bryant said. *"But I never lost faith. I prayed on the subject and knew God would lead me and Wesley House in the right direction."* That night, Bryant woke up at 3 a.m. and went downstairs to the living room. *"Most nights I wake up and go right back to sleep. This night, I was called downstairs to read my Bible."* He opened to the Book of Nehemiah and read about Nehemiah's struggle between remaining as the

Validation

cupbearer to the king of Persia and being called by God to lead the rebuilding of the walls of Jerusalem. Seeing obvious parallels to his own struggles with decision-making regarding assuming the leadership of Wesley House, Bryant knew God was leading him to embrace the challenge. *"It was really eerie; one of those hair-raising experiences,"* Bryant said of the night. *"I threw my name into the national search the next day, and three weeks later, the job was mine. It was meant to be."* Bryant, who had previously held director positions on interim basis with the Omaha Minority Contractors Association and Urban League of Omaha, was greeted two days before taking the reins at Wesley House with an immediate concern that made him question his decision – but never his commitment.

"I met the board chairman for lunch, and he alerted me that the organization had $40,000 in debt that wasn't on the financial sheets I originally saw," Bryant said. *"It raised immediate red flags, and I asked myself, "Should I take this job after all? "But*

Validation

when I thought about it, I realized this was bigger than me and $40,000. This was an opportunity to plant seeds that will change kids' lives for the better and I wanted to be an active part of the solution."

One of his first acts as the new executive director was to set a 40-day timeline to wipe out the $40,000 in debt. With mostly $25 and $50 donations along with a few $1,000 gifts, he eliminated the financial albatross in 36 days. *"I saw many Biblical analogies in the $40,000 debt – Moses and the Jews wandering the desert for 40 years, Noah and the floods that lasted 40 days and 40 nights – and he knew that we could overcome it and God world provide."* Bryant said.

Getting Wesley House on solid financial ground is a mission he will continue to champion along with building young people with impeccable manners, strong business smarts and passion for a brighter future – something they most likely would have imagined or planned for without Wesley House.

337

Validation

"Not one day goes by when I don't thank God for leading me in the direction," Bryant said, despite working in somewhat dilapidated conditions compared to what he was used to in the corporate world. *"As a former collegiate athlete, I've always been extremely competitive, and that competitive fire drives me today in leading Wesley House to a place of prominence and purpose it deserves." "I tell our 105-strong kids that smart people win, and it's my mission to see that kids in North Omaha realize they can win with their minds as well as with their legs and arms and hands."*

Things people say about you while you now are the very things they will embellish when you are dead. Live each day like there is no tomorrow, sing like no one is listening and dance like no one is looking… You live your legacy everyday.

"I can't hear what you say because what you do speaks so loudly."

- Unknown

Chapter Sixteen

Honesty

Can <u>you</u> stand to hear the truth?

> *"If you throw a rock into a pack of dogs, the one that yelps, is the one that got hit!"*
>
> *-Old African Proverb*

Leaders must have the strength, courage and confidence to tell the truth even when they are saying things people may not want to hear. Honesty is a cornerstone of Purpose Living Leadership.

There are messages for society that need to be delivered; things that need to be said. I feel compelled to speak out, if I don't, who will? If I don't say something now, when will it be said? Maybe the whole point of writing this book was to remind people that the foundation for humanity is built on eternal footings.

340

Honesty

An everlasting God, in his image, created us and we yearn to be with him like a child yearns to be with its mother. Like a freshly hatched Sea Turtle that immediately begins to scamper toward the ocean, humans are naturally drawn toward eternity.

No one with a sound mind or a healthy body wants to die. We are constantly looking at ways to stay healthier; we exercise, we monitor our diets and we visit the doctor regularly. All these things we do in order to live longer. Our obsession with living is understandable. Something within us desires to be reunited with our maker.

We will never be content until we are reconciled with our creator. We try to fill this void with possessions, but the things of this world never quite satisfy our feelings of incompleteness. Regardless of what we accomplish we will always want more. The bible says, *"All Rivers run into the sea, yet the sea is never full; the eye is not satisfied with seeing nor the ear satisfied with hearing."*

Honesty

In this wonderful age of technology, far too many people have no relationship with God. For most of them, nothing is more important than accumulating the wealth of this world. Society's mantra says, *"If it feels good do it!"* This is the message we are constantly being fed through the movies, music and television. Is it any surprise that Money, Sex and Power are the top three reasons for the demise of our leaders and our families?

Here's the secret: <u>You will never be satisfied with earthly treasures.</u> No matter what you achieve or what you accomplish, you will always want more. True fulfillment does not come from accumulating money or power; it comes from having an intimate relationship with God and working toward your purpose. To me, an intimate relationship entails multiple interactions with God on a daily basis. I acknowledge him daily for the simple things; the morning dew, the warmth of the sun, the beauty of nature or friendly smiles. I thank him constantly for my family and our health. I know everything I have

Honesty

is a gift from him and he has given me more than I deserve. This knowledge has inspired me to try and do the right thing, (I'm not perfect) and to tell others about him.

Society will continue to slide toward an inevitable demise if we don't recognize the source of that internal desire for eternity. Sooner or later, we all come to grips with our mortality. This sobering reality comes to us most often as we age. This is a major reason behind the contributions many rich people make toward capital campaigns. Having their name on a building is a way for them to obtain a sliver of immortality; their legacy. The bible says *"both the rich man and the poor man have this in common; the grave."*

No rational person wants to die. Give the wealthiest people in the world their choice of eternal life or their names on a building; I'll wager they choose life... Give them eternal life and most of them will totally forget about their legacies.

Honesty

The greatest legacy in history involves a poor leader who was Honest with the people. He told them many things they didn't want to hear and he was killed because he refused to water down his message. It's a classic story of love and trust between a father and son. It has a very relevant and powerful message for today because so many young people grow up fatherless.

When the Father realized man was incapable of achieving salvation, he developed a plan to pardon humanity. His divine strategy required an accomplice, someone he could trust to share the **vision** of his plan; someone who believed in the **purpose** for saving humanity. He needed someone with the **courage** to remain faithful, in the midst of tribulations and the **perseverance** to carry out the mission, even though it would have a tragic conclusion. He could have selected a king or one of the prophets, but the Father chose his son.

Honesty

Jesus was equipped with everything he needed to complete his task and his father stood with him every step of the way. Knowing God would never leave him strengthened Jesus' resolve; he maintained his **faith** in the plan even though he knew he would suffer. He trusted his father and he knew God would be there for him at the end. He has given **Hope** to billions of people that they may one day be reconciled with God. Because of Jesus' obedience, two thousand years later, his **influence** is felt around the world.

A good father has a natural desire to impart wisdom and knowledge into his children. There is an unexplainable and unique relationship between a father and his offspring. Children are like the portal through which a father can achieve immortality; it is through his children that a father establishes a legacy. If you raise good children; who needs a building?

Honesty

Jesus' assignment was great, yet amazingly simple: to save humanity. His mission is summed up in an often quoted scripture in the bible, John 3:16. *"For God so loved the world that He gave His only begotten Son, that whoever believes in Him should not perish, but have eternal life."*

It has been said, *"Without a vision, the people will perish."* Most often vision comes from our leaders. My prayer is for this new day; this time of change to usher in a new style of leader in Government, Business, and our Families. The brand of leader who knows true happiness comes from having joy in your heart, purpose in your step and passion for what you do. We need leaders who will be examples that truly successful people know the creator, find their purpose and work diligently every day to accomplish their mission.

A Purpose Living Leader has a **Vision** for where they want to go and an altruistic **Purpose** for reaching that destination. **Courage** is a must

346

because pursuing their vision will lead them to the road less traveled. **Perseverance** is what's needed to stay the course when the road gets rough and opposition surfaces. **Faith** is an unwavering belief in success and it empowers them to persist without quitting. **Hope** is future focused faith; to look forward with unwavering optimism. And **Influence,** the most important element of leadership, should always be used for the betterment of mankind...

ORDER ADDITIONAL COPIES TODAY!

The Purpose-Living Leader

Please send _____ copies of The Purpose-Living Leader by Paul E. Bryant @ $20.00 / copy + $5.00 Shipping and Handling. Free S&H for orders of 10 or more books. I have enclosed a check or money order, made payable to the "Leadership Institute for Urban Education" in the amount of $ _____

Mail to: Leadership Institute for Urban Education

2605 North 32nd Avenue

Omaha, Nebraska 68111

Website: www.thelegacyofleadership.com

Name		
Address		
City	State / Province	
Zip / Postal Code	Phone	
Email Address		

About the Author

Paul Bryant is an experienced voice of leadership in Urban America. He is the Founder of the Leadership Institute for Urban Education, Executive Director of UMCC Wesley House Leadership Academy and a Board Member of Leadership for Life. He holds Masters Degrees in both Urban Studies and Urban Education. Paul previously served as the Interim President and CEO of the Urban League of Nebraska, President and CEO of the United Minority Contractors Association and Host for the weekly radio program "Inside Urban America."

Paul's corporate career includes a Senior Vice President post with The Gallup Organization, and Business Banker and Officer positions with Wells Fargo and the First National Bank.

Paul received the Martin Luther King "Living the Dream" Award and the University of Nebraska's Alumnus Achievement Award. He was named the "Facilitator of the Year" by INROADS Inc, a Black Achiever by the YMCA, and an Achiever to Watch in the Millennium Success Guide. Paul was a member of Leadership Omaha and was named one of the Ten Outstanding Young Omahans by the Junior Chamber of Commerce.

Paul believes, *"The best way to rebuild a community is to invest in its future Leaders."*

Special thanks to the American and Peoples National Banks and to John and Wende Kotouc. Your generosity has paved the way for the Purpose Living Leader. God bless you for your support and your belief in this project.